Walk with Me

By Mark Lynch

TATE PUBLISHING, LLC

"Walk with Me" by Mark Lynch
Copyright © 2005 by Mark Lynch. All rights reserved.

Published in the United States of America
by Tate Publishing, LLC
127 East Trade Center Terrace
Mustang, OK 73064
(888) 361–9473

Book design copyright © 2005 by Tate Publishing, LLC. All rights reserved.

No part of this publication may be reproduced, stored in a retrieval system or transmitted in any way by any means, electronic, mechanical, photocopy, recording or otherwise without the prior permission of the author except as provided by USA copyright law.

Scripture quotations marked "NIV" are taken from the Holy Bible, New International Version ®, Copyright © 1973, 1978, 1984 by International Bible Society. Used by permission of Zondervan Publishing House. All rights reserved.

ISBN: 1–59886–10–5-0

Dedication

I first and foremost dedicate this book to my Lord and Savior Jesus Christ. I also dedicate this book to the memory of my Grandmother Lucy. Although she has past from this world "she is" one of the greatest woman I have ever known. She is no stranger to God and I will be with her again one day; of that I am sure. She always had a heart full of love and compassion. She gave her love freely and in return she is loved by all ten of her children, her children's spouses and her many grandchildren. She is and always will be loved by anyone her life touched. I will always remember how she would always put a coin in my hand in exchange for kiss and a hug. In hind sight I now see how Jesus lived through her and what it means to be a Christian. When she passed on it was more than I could bare and I thought I would die. She was the biggest influence in my life. I didn't know it then, but God would give me Ag for my wife. Ag is so very much like my Nana Lucy.

Table of Contents

Preface.. 7
Foreword.. 9
The Front Cover 11
Chapter 1: Getting to Know Me 13
Chapter 2: The Lynch Mob............................ 17
Chapter 3: Bullies, Trouble and Revenge............ 23
Chapter 4: The Relatives and Lazy Summers........ 29
Chapter 5: Harry.. 31
Chapter 6: Puberty..................................... 33
Chapter 7: Life on the Streets........................ 37
Chapter 8: My Aggy..................................... 45
Chapter 9: Employment................................ 49
Chapter 10: School..................................... 53
Chapter 11: The Wheels................................ 55
Chapter 12: Beyond the Call of Duty................. 59
Chapter 13: The Ice.................................... 65
Chapter 14: The Damage 69
Chapter 15: The Bank Robbery 75
Chapter 16: PTSD and Twins 79
Chapter 17: Our Twins 83
Chapter 18: The Encounter with God 87
Chapter 19: My New Business 93
Chapter 20: My Cousin Brian.......................... 97
Chapter 21: My Adriana 101
Chapter 22: Darwin's Joke 105
Chapter 23: Various Beliefs 109
Chapter 24: Jewish or Muslim 113
Chapter 25: Roman Catholic Traditions 119
Chapter 26: The Truth................................. 129
Chapter 27: Feeding the Seed 131
Chapter 28: The Accident 137
Chapter 29: The Struggle 143
Chapter 30: A Miracle.................................. 147

Chapter 31: Our Son Marc 151
Chapter 32: Our Son John........................... 155
Chapter 33: The First Time I Died 165
Chapter 34: The Second Time I Died 171
Chapter 35: It's All About Relationships 177
Chapter 36: Reason and Choice 183
Chapter 37: The Sacrifice 187
Chapter 38: Developing the Relationship................. 191
Chapter 39: There Is a Reason 197
Chapter 40: Someplace Worse Than Hell................. 201
Chapter 41: Live by What You Believe 205
Chapter 42: Talking to God........................... 209
Chapter 43: Child-like Faith.......................... 213
Chapter 44: My Soul Mate 215
Chapter 45: The Tattoo.............................. 219
Chapter 46: In Conclusion 223

Preface

I have no intention of plagiarizing anyone in writing this book. I stand beside my many true brothers and sisters in scattering seed. This book is my personal testimony. I want to share my personal witness of the experiences, knowledge, understanding and words God has shared with me. The theology in my book has been around for thousands of years. Some of the words I have to share you may have heard preached from a pulpit, read in a book or heard from a minister or from a friend. Sometimes we hear without really listening. Sometimes someone will tell us something and we never hear them. Then someone else will come along and tell us the very same thing. We may not really pay attention the first time we hear something. It may have to be repeated or said differently a second or third time before we really hear and get the message loud and clear. As long as the reader gets this message and it helps in advancing Glory to God, then my goal is achieved. I have found many people need information broken down so that they can understand it better. I have taught quite a number of people including professing "Christians" over the years who never knew a lot about what they professed to be their belief. I have also found quite a number of people who hang on to their beliefs simply out of tradition. These people have never really given any serious thought about what or why they believe as they do; it was just the way they were taught or brought up by their family.

Teaching is more than just knowing and understanding your subject matter. You have to be able to explain information to others in a way that they too can know, understand and apply the information. I believe the experiences of my life and the people placed in my life, along with the gifts of understanding and teaching are all from God. The gifts I have been given are to be used to help others. I strongly believe my most cherished friend wants me to write this book. His name is Jesus. I also believe that I was not allowed to remain in paradise when I died, as this book needed to be written. I firmly believe that I am to write this book as a witness who is attempting to point as many people as possible to the right path in this life. My most treasured prayer is that one day I will hear Jesus tell me, "Well done my good and faithful servant." I am writing this book not to glorify myself but to place all the glory where it belongs, "on God alone." I am attempting to illustrate through glimpses of my life and through personal experiences how God has guided and changed me. How God has given me a new nature. When I was young I "knew of God." I now "know God," yet not completely. When I was young I lived a "me" centered life. God has shown and taught me how to "really live" is to live a "God" centered life. As I share parts of my life the reader can see how God has worked in my life. God allows certain circumstances and people to enter our lives to mold us into the person we are to become. Now I cannot even fathom living any part of life without God.

Foreword

Mark and Agnes Lynch are the real deal. They are serious about their commitment to Christ and they live out what they believe. I've been privileged to know them as their Pastor and their friend for the last 14 years.

"Walk with Me" is Mark's powerful testimony, his story of how he came to know and trust in Jesus Christ as his Lord. It's his story, so it's unique to him, as you will see. Our God is a God of infinite variety, so every Christian's faith journey will be somewhat different. Mark's life experiences are extraordinary and fascinating. In knowing Mark and after finishing Mark's book, I commented that the name of the book should be changed to "Job the Sequel."

It really doesn't matter so much how we come to trust in Christ; what matters is that we eventually truly turn to him to receive his forgiveness and life as it was always meant to be. Mark carefully avoids the use of Christian jargon words in his story, which makes for a good read. It's a story you won't soon forget, and who knows? You might find some unexpected benefits in this book.

Rev. Robert A. Killeffer, Jr.
First Baptist Church
Braintree, MA.

The Front Cover

The front cover is a picture that I took around 1970 in the Boston Common near the intersection of Beacon Street and Charles Street. I thought it was a good picture of a tender moment where here is this rough-looking guy walking through the Common with this little child hand in hand.

Getting to know me

Chapter 1

I have always been more of a non-conformist and a bit of a rebel. I have a problem in blindly following others and instead choose to take control. I am not easily swayed and need to ponder the facts. I want the reader to get to know me, if only a little. My friends who do know me have prodded me to reveal even more of myself beyond this book, how they see me and know me.

    I heard it said that you cannot judge a book by its cover. When I enter a store or restaurant I get the usual lines. When I had my moustache people would often stop me and ask if I am Dennis Frantz: the guy on the TV program NYPD. I shaved off my moustache and now people think I'm Tony Soprano. It's been asked of me more than once if I am a Mafia mob boss or if I kill people for a living. Seeing me is not the same as knowing me. I need the reader to see beyond the external to my heart and soul. I want to share parts of my life in order that the reader can begin to know me, the real me, inside the outer shell. I also want to attempt to show the changes in me as I grew. I realize some of the changes are due from the natural maturing process. It's more than that though. I know that I now live in God and God lives in me. God always was and still is in control of the events in my life. When I was younger I believed in a distant, untouchable God. I believed that "if" there really was a God he would be watching over the earth from a distance and he never would be able see any detail from his distant viewing point. I was certain he could not see anything in the dark, nor could he see anything hidden. I never really believed that God would see or know everything or everybody. I never thought that God was a personal God that not only knows everybody; but he also knows everybody's thoughts and actions. When I was young God was not in me, nor was I in God. There is a big difference between knowing "of" someone and actually getting to know someone.

I have found many people who believe that they are and profess to be Christians, are in reality not true Christians at all. I was once as they are. Quite a number of these people come from a number of mainline religious organizations. These people have never discovered what it means to be what God considers someone who is "chosen" or a "true Christian." God's ways are not our ways. God says what he means and means what he says. God does not think as humans do; his thoughts are infinitely higher than our thoughts. God thinks on a much higher plain; he sees a bigger picture. As humans we are limited in what we can see or understand. To become one of his "chosen," or a true Christian, requires a person to have a personal relationship with God. This means that you need to know God, not simply to know of God. In order to have this personal relationship you must be "born again" from above. I will explain this in detail a little later on in this book. Some people believe if they belong to a religious organization, or attend a church, every day, every week, or just for Christmas and Easter, or if they repeat particular well-known prayers over and over again that this will count in God's eyes as proof they are Christians and get them into heaven when they pass on from this world. I want to show the reader that this is not what God is looking for. I know these people who think they are Christians are something else, "according to God." Our personal opinions about this do not matter in the end. We are all just clay and God is the Potter. The clay does not get to tell the Potter the rules. God is looking for those who are chosen and seek a relationship with him. God is not seeking those that simply belong to any particular religion. I will also explain this in basic detail further in this book. As I take the reader through my life, please notice that I am no one special. I am just an average person, a mostly C student. My father would often tell me that I would never amount to much in this life. But, God chooses and changes people. All of the people who were God inspired and wrote the wildly accepted Bible were just average people. They were not born with supernatural abilities. Yet every one of them had this relationship with God that I am writing about. They all were just ordinary people that were indwelt by God or inspired by God in what they wrote and did. They all found God and He lead them to the truth. They all were helped by God and He changed their lives. They all knew God and are all with God. When God entered my life I was like a filthy rag, not a white clean cloth; as you will see as I tell my story. God has cleaned me up a bit; but he is not done with me yet.

I would like to share parts of my life and some of the extreme situations I had to experience and endure for what was given to me by God. Hopefully I will be able to convey my story in a simple, understandable manner and the reader will better understand the message I am attempting to convey in this book.

The Lynch Mob and Relatives

Chapter 2

My mother's younger brother, my uncle Vinny (yes I really have an uncle Vinny), used to tease me often because I'm left handed. He used to tell me that lefty's can't do anything right. But research has proven otherwise. Right-handed people mainly use the left side of their brains as left-handed people use the right side of their brain. I have also heard it said left-handed people are the only people functioning in their right mind. All I know is that I see things from a different angle than most people. In all honesty I don't know if it has anything to do with being left handed or not. Writing a book is not easy for me. I will confess I was a C student when it came to anything that had to do with English. I never was a big fan of books or newspapers. I'm the kind of guy that will wait for the movie to come out and watch the news occasionally on TV. I am a Math and Science person as opposed to an English scholar.

In reading about parts of my life the reader will see that I have faced struggles that I would not wish on my enemies. I have dealt with physical and emotional pain far beyond that of the average person. I am also well acquainted with death. I also know what it is like to be so emotionally scared and so depressed that suicide appears as a good alternative. I attempted suicide on several occasions only to have my efforts thwarted.

Many, many times in my life I have wondered, "Why me?" I eventually found that there is a reason for everything in life, though many times I did not understand. I hope that you can see from my experiences that through it all that, no matter how hard the struggle, you still must go on. As for me, I found that this can only be done with God's help. You have to play the cards you're dealt and live the life that was given to you. You must always remember that a piece of coal put under tremendous pressure produces a diamond. Find God and with his help you can beat life's struggles and become the diamond.

When I was young, my paternal grandfather Pete used to practice daily on me using what I used to call the 50 cent words; now they are more like $1000 words. You know the big, impressive words that are in the dictionary, but the average person has never heard them, spoken them, or wouldn't know, or care to know what they mean. I think he was always just trying to impress me. Other people might have been impressed, but I wasn't. Instead, I felt Pete had a problem. I think the use of $1000 words is more self-serving to the individual using them. I feel they are used by individuals who have some "superiority need" or false sense of self-importance. Actually I feel that using $1000 words are more of a handicap. In the real world, instead of impressing a minority people of how "all knowing" you are of the English language, it actually isolates you from the majority, as the majority don't have a clue about what you are saying. So as you read on please pardon me if I don't use many $1000 words.

I grew up in a suburb of Boston. I am the second oldest of seven. I have an older sister and I had a younger sister. Her name was Lori. My sister Lori passed away at a very early age. It's hard to talk about and even harder to write about, so I'm just going to leave it at that for now. My brothers are Peter, John, Matthew and Luke. I bet you heard those names before, maybe not in that order. My father is Irish, German and very Roman Catholic. My family wasn't wealthy, but all our needs were provided for. My father was a full-time school teacher and a part-time bookkeeper for a local theatre owner.

My father didn't smoke, drink nor abandon my mother and us children. When he wasn't working he would be home helping my mom. He did the best he could to provide for us all. I was proud of him being a school teacher. I also used to think it was a good thing that he worked as a bookkeeper. We got to see a lot of free movies while my father worked upstairs in the office of the theatre. For the most part my mother stayed home while we were young and then she worked part-time at a department store when we were older. My mother is all Italian, supposedly a Roman Catholic, but not a practicing Roman Catholic. Often I would hear her say the Pope was nothing but a poop. I cannot recall her ever attending church and often wondered why I had to.

Starting out, my family lived in a six room, three bedroom and one bath second floor apartment. Peter, John, Matt and I all shared a 9' by 12' bedroom, fully equipped with two bunk beds and one four drawer chest. Each of us was supposed to have our own drawer. It never worked out that way and we were always wearing each others' clothes. We considered all clothes community property until we outgrew them. Then all clothes were shipped out to our younger cousins. Meal time was interesting. First come, first served. If you were late you got whatever was left. My siblings and I were shown by my parents that life is a competition and only the strong survive. I have also learned from growing up on the streets, the way to really know if people are speaking the truth is by watching them. Through their actions the truth is revealed. Actions speak so much louder than words. What people do will reveal how they really feel and think. Words are easy to come by.

Now let's talk about love. I love the Patriots, cool summer breezes, chocolate cake and my wife and children. Love is a word that gets thrown around a lot. I don't love my wife and kids in the same way I love chocolate cake. The seeds that were planted in me by my mother and father were not seeds of love. My siblings and I had to strive for either Mom or Dad's approval or disapproval of us in a competition. I recall many times as a child hearing my mother say, "Get away from me" or, "Stop hanging on me." I also clearly remember my father's words to me. He would constantly call me "lard ass" or "pain in the ass." I still hear his words telling me that I would never amount to anything. Growing up, I can never recall ever hearing the words "I love you" from either of my parents. I cannot recall ever being kissed or hugged by either of my parents. My siblings and I would always be compared to one another by our parents. I would often here my father say to me, "Why couldn't you be more like your older sister or your younger brother Peter." It wasn't really abuse; it just wasn't good and it certainly wasn't warm, fuzzy, cuddly expressed love.

My parents would occasionally display more of an open physical love toward each other. The only warm expressed love I ever received and felt came from my grandmother. I just figured my parents were not capable of showing love to their children. I really didn't miss then, what I didn't really know should have existed. My father also has always had a sick jealousy thing. He did not like my mother paying any special attention to me and he really got his hemorrhoids in an uproar when I started to develop a relationship with my younger sister Lori.

I remember one day after Ag and I had been married for some time going over my brother Peter's house for a birthday party. My wife Agnes was with me as I wanted her to witness what was going to be said as I was about to approach my father. I walked up to my father who was sitting on a chair in the back yard. I said, "Dad, I want to ask you something. My whole life I have always felt that you didn't care for me much and that you rejected me."

I will never forget his reply. He said, "You're right, and I still do." This was just another seed he would plant in my mind.

Ours was not a healthy, loving parent / child relationship. My family more closely resembled what you would find in raising competitive pit bulls than you find with a normal family. It was and still is a dysfunctional family. The result of our upbringing or the harvest from the planted seeds: my brothers and sister are not very close to each other. We only meet on rare occasions. We don't hang around each other. We rarely call each other and we don't get involved in each others lives. I do care about my parents and my siblings; but I can't say that it is love. My dad worked very hard to provide for all of our physical needs, not our wants, nor our psychological or emotional needs (for sure not mine). I know it was a handful for my parents raising seven children. I respect both my mother and my father for providing for all of our physical needs. Yet, I made myself a vow that I would never raise my children the same way. Each of my children will always be told and reminded that I love them. Each and every one of them is the most precious jewel I have. I would never pit them against each other. I will also be careful of the seeds I sow in them.

Bullies, Trouble and Revenge

Chapter 3

Other than my dysfunctional family, life wasn't too bad growing up. Not too many overwhelming obstacles. I liked to horse around and joke. I was vainly full of myself. Most always I would have a smile on my face. When I joked around I would make my mother laugh her approval and I would make my father scowl showing his disapproval. I liked being physical. I loved playing baseball, basketball and football. I also wasn't one that could be easily intimidated and would never back down from a conflict. After a few well won skirmishes with the neighborhood boys, they knew me well enough not to give me a hard time. I never went out looking for a problem or a fight. I just didn't care for bullies. I thought of myself as the hero to the underdog and a tough kid. I learned a good left hook, or well thrown elbow or foot could settle problems quickly. I found it an advantage being left handed, as my opponent would rarely see the left hook coming.

I remember these two boys that lived next door to us. They were a couple of bullies that I never cared for. They would always pick on my younger brothers and the neighborhood kids that were smaller than them. One of these boys was a little older than me and the other one was a few months younger than me. Both of them were about my same size. I remember one time the two of them were in their yard throwing tomatoes at my house and saying some really nasty things about my mother. They were trying to get me to lose my temper and they knew they were safe as I wasn't allowed to go after them in their yard. I wasn't one to let anything go by and knew I would get revenge at the right time. I waited and got each one separately when they came home from school. I gave them each a good beating.

Then one winter day as I was coming home from my grandmother's house these same two boys were both hiding in some bushes that I had to pass by. They jumped out of their hiding place and knocked me over. Then they both took turns sitting on me. As one of them would hold me down, the other one would kick and punch me. If I started to break free they both would jump on me and hold me down. They had this old sheep dog they named Daisy. They called Daisy over to lick my face while they were sitting on me. They were also putting snow on my face and down my shirt. I was furious! I finally knocked them both over and they ran into their house. They had shut and locked the storm door. I was now in a rage and this time they were going to pay big! Forget any rules. I picked up a trash can and flung it at their storm door, shattering the glass. I then reached in and unlocked the door and ran up their stairs after them. They could not believe what I did as they both ran for cover. One boy, the older one, went out on their back porch. I hit him as hard as I could and then kicked him several times between his legs as he fell to the deck. He was screaming now, bent in a ball of pain, so I then turned my attention to his younger brother. His brother just made it out of the house when I lunged on him. I remember beating him and then grabbing him by both ears and smashing the back of his head onto the street curb. There was a lot of blood, but I was still furious and wasn't planning to stop.

My uncle Vinny and my older sister had heard the commotion by now and came running out of my house. My sister was hitting me with a broom as my uncle jumped on top of me trying to pull me off this kid in attempting to get me to stop.

If they didn't stop me I probably would have killed the kid. The police were called, but when the whole story came out the mother of the boys decided not to press any charges. I remember her sitting me on the stairs of their house and the mother just talked to me about the forgiveness of Jesus. I was polite but I wasn't really listening to her. I was just relieved that the police were out of the picture. I wasn't sorry for anything I had done and was still furious with those two boys. In my eyes it still was not over.

I always seemed to manage to get into mischief and somehow my older sister would always find out. She was Daddy's little girl and a squealer. Whenever I did something wrong she would run and tell Daddy. She would always stand right next to him while I was getting screamed at. She would wiggle her little head and stick her tongue out at me, savoring every minute at my expense. Sometimes she would even make up lies about something I never did and I would still be blamed and punished. My father would always take her side, every time. In his eyes his little angel could do no wrong and I was nothing but trouble. Believe me, she is no angel. I do know how to get even though.

I remember one time we had a rodent problem. My father bought this great mouse trap that could catch at least 4 mice at the same time. I would get up early, all excited, then run over to check the trap and see what was caught. One morning there were 2 dead mice, one tail without a mouse attached to it and a fourth mouse that was caught by its tail. The fourth mouse was still alive. Wow, this was great! I quickly got a jar. I put holes in the lid, put in a little grass and put in the mouse that was still alive. I had plans for this mouse. I kept him in the cellar until Sunday evening. Sunday evening was bath night. After the boys were done bathing, it would be the girls' turn. While the girls were in the tub I could sneak in their room and do my thing. Sunday night was when I would usually get my revenge for my sisters squealing. Maybe I chose bath night because it had something to do with me knowing that my sister wasn't so squeaky clean. I got the mouse and tucked him nicely under my sister's blankets so he couldn't escape. Yah, I knew I would get screamed at, but it would be worth any punishment just hearing her scream. I waited up as long as I could but my sister never screamed. In fact, to my amazement, nothing happened that night. The next morning I remember checking under the blankets of my sister's bed after she had gotten up looking for that mouse. I never found the mouse. The mouse had really disappointed me. Another time I caught a garter snake and I put it in her pillow. The same thing happened. No screams and no snake! I never thought about the mouse and the snake escaping.

As for my brothers, I was the oldest and whenever anyone gave them a hard time they knew they could count on me to come to their aid and rescue them from whoever was picking on them. We did have our sibling rivalry though. I remember this one time when my younger brother Peter was digging for worms in the garden. He had been really getting on my nerves. He was digging with a pitch fork. We were arguing about something stupid. I said something he didn't like, so he threw the pitch fork at me. I got out of the way just in time, but now I was mad and picked up the pitch fork and put it through his foot. He had to get a few stitches and a tetanus shot. Of course, I was the only one who got punished. I wasn't the least bit sorry.

My next youngest brother was John. John, putting it nicely, was weird. In fact we nick named him "weird-o." He had this "thing" about iodine. He would always be painting his body with it, saying he was covering mosquito bites. He was as skinny as a stick and had this wild hair that stood out like an afro hairstyle even though he was mostly Italian. He was into bugs and bug torture. John loved the neighbor's cat and was always carrying it. The cat had most of its hair missing and was loaded with sores. Most everyone wouldn't even approach this cat, never mind pick it up and carry it. John also liked fire. One day I was supposed to be watching my younger brothers and sister while my mom and my older sister ran out for a minute to do something. While I was watching TV with my brothers and sister I started to smell smoke. I went out to the kitchen to see John lighting newspapers off the stove and then throwing them still lit into the plastic waste barrel. The barrel was burning, as was the rear wall of the house. I ran out the front door screaming, "Women and children first," as my older sister and my mom had just returned. My mom and sister got the fire out just as the firemen had shown up. Of course, I got the blame for that one too. John needed "pay back" for this one as I got into trouble because of something he did. I just had to wait for the right time.

My father had hay fever and every week he would go to the doctor for a shot. Since I was grounded from the pitch fork incident with my brother Peter, I had to go with my father when he went to the doctor. I had to wait in the car with my younger brother John, who was also grounded for calling my mother a bitch. John was also a whiner. He just went on and on with his whining. He was planning to run out of the car and run down the street, which would get me into more trouble. I had enough of John and it was time for the pay back. As he opened the door to get out, I jumped out of the front door and grabbed him. I then threw him back into the car. As he tried to get out again I slammed the door shut. Of course his fingers were not all the way in at the time. They saved his fingers, but his finger nails never grew back right, and yeah, I got it for that one too. I felt worse for me than I did for my brother.

I never had any incident with my other younger brothers, Matthew and Luke; they we too small at the time. My brother Matthew is very sensitive and emotional. He can make a mountain out of a mole hill. Despite his opinion to the contrary, I do not recall picking on him much. I always liked my baby brother Luke. I used to get up nights and help either my mother or father change his diapers or feed him. After a few unwelcomed yellow showers I learned to be quick putting on a diaper.

I also liked my little sister Lori. However, there was a time when I ran into a little problem with my little sister. I was supposed to be baby sitting her while my parents went to the store. I had to entertain her and keep her occupied. She liked it when I swung her around by her arms. She kept asking me to swing her around. So I held her hands and started to swing her around. She was laughing as I swung her around and around. Then all of sudden I heard these cracking, popping sounds. Suddenly her arms were like jello and now she was screaming! I knew something was wrong and I was now in big trouble. I tried to get her to be quiet but it wasn't working. So I brought her upstairs and put her in her closet. I shut the door on her and took off, knowing my parents would be home at any minute. What can I say; it was a really dumb move. I was more worried about what was going to happen to me than I was about my sister. I needed a head start to get away. I didn't get far, as my parents pulled up. Well at least I learned that you don't swing little kids around by their arms. Both of her arms were pulled out of their sockets. There were a lot more little incidences like this with me. As I got a little older, I found it better for me not to be home so much; that way fewer things seemed to happen. I also knew I was rejected and it was better for me to stay away anyway.

The Relatives and Lazy Summers

Chapter 4

I would spend a lot of time with my cousins, mostly with my cousins on my mother's side of the family. I probably have hundreds of cousins, most of which I don't even know. Their parents would usually get many of us together at whatever house Uncle Vinny would be giving haircuts. There would be anywhere from a half dozen of us to a dozen or more getting Uncle Vinny's military style "whiffle" haircut. It didn't take long to realize that you did not want to be Uncle Vinny's first victim in the haircut line. That poor soul would be Uncle Vinny's warm-up victim. That was the individual who would receive the most head gouges. I also learned not to be at the end of the line as the electric hair clipper was more like an electric branding iron. You never knew at what time Uncle Vinny was going to draw blood, what was going to be cut off, or permanently branded. I can still see him tossing those clippers from one hand to the next, blowing on the clippers trying to cool them down. Sometimes the clippers would even end up in the ice box for quick cool down.

By the time I was ten most of my time was spent hanging out with my cousin Dave. We would both hang out with the same gang of kids. Dave and I were about the same age. Dave's parents, my Aunt Lola (my mother's sister) and my Uncle Joe, had a cottage on Cape Cod. I spent a lot of weekends and most of the summer there when I was between the ages of 10 and 14. My Aunt and Uncle were always kind to me. I can remember all the times that my Aunt Lola would make me as many pancakes or English muffins as I could eat. She never complained and never scolded me. I also thought she was a great cook and my mouth waters even now remembering everything she cooked for me. She would take the special care to be sure to bring us to the beach, the drive in, the penny candy store, or Howard Johnson's Ice Cream Parlor. She didn't have to do this, she just did it. Next to my Nana this woman will always be very special to me!

Harry

Chapter 5

By the time I had become a teenager our little group of friends had grown. I had become part of a fairly large gang of kids that "socialized" together. Most of my time was spent hanging out on a street corner with these kids. We definitely weren't angels, but I didn't think we were all that bad. I guess it would depend on what standard we were measured from. We used to hang across from this little variety store. It was owned and run by this old Armenian guy named Harry. Harry rarely shaved and always looked like he had never taken a bath in his life. He wore the same old clothes everyday. His store would always smell like sardines. All he had in his store was junk food, a few bottles of milk, some bread, some sodas and cigarettes. I remember asking him why he even bothered to stay in business, why didn't he just retire. He told me in broken English that if you stop work, you die.

Harry was a grumpy, irritable, cantankerous old man. If you didn't have the right change for something you were buying, he would usually start swearing at you and throw you out of his store. He would snap at the drop of a dime. He had his own whacked out rules. Most of the kids I hung around were not allowed in his store. They would taunt him, constantly, just to get him swearing. Sometimes one or two of the guys would climb up on his roof and start jumping on it. He would come out of the store fuming! He would always be screaming the same thing in broken English, "You - sum- of- a- bitchen- bastads- you! I killa-you, you dirty bastards - you!" As Harry would run around the back of his store a couple of the kids would run in his front door and steal as many cartons of cigarettes that they could carry.

I tried not to get on Harry's bad side though, because I wanted to be able to buy his junk food and cigarettes. I learned that it's easier to be nice to people. This was not because I was nice, but because I never knew when I might need them. I wasn't worried about Harry; I was only thinking of my own interests. The nearest store was a long walk away from Harry's and Harry would sell cigarettes to 10 year olds. Harry also had a great collection of porn magazines. Only the privileged few were allowed to view and buy them. Harry had poor eyesight and was really into stocks. Everyday he would be hunched over with his glasses on and a big magnifying glass in his hand reading the stock pages in the paper. If I came in his store alone he would have me find and read different stock prices to him. For doing this Harry would give me free candy bars and allow me access to his magazine collection as long as I didn't tell anyone. See, being nice pays off. I did it all for the "what's" in it for me.

Puberty

Chapter 6

I remember the time a couple of friends and I came across a whole stack of porn magazines some guy was throwing out. We thought we had found the pot of gold at the end of the rainbow. I think we were 13 years old at the time. We quickly ran to the woods next to my house where we stashed them. There we could enjoy them while we smoked our cigarettes. I remember I took a few of the better magazines and hid them under my mattress for private fantasy viewing. I also remember when I went to get them I found that my bed was made up. Where I had put the magazines, now was a note. It read, "What are you, taking up art now?" signed, "your Mother!" She never said anything else about it and I wasn't about to say anything about it.

When I was young, girls were always of interest to me; they always caught my eye. Girls gave me that good tingling feeling, made my head swim, made me stutter and always had my full attention, if you know what I mean. I wasn't interested in girls as people. I thought of them as objects that could relieve my sexual desires. I thought of girls for what they did for me. I liked to do the chasing; it had to be a conquest, a notch in my belt. I felt uncomfortable when the girls would chase me, never thinking that girls could think of boys the same way boys would think of girls. This all changed when I actually fell in love. It changed even more when I eventually had a house full of daughters. Both instances eventually woke me up to reality and I now see women in an entirely different light.

I started working when I was 11 years old. I had a paper route and would caddy at a golf course on the weekends. When I turned 14 years old I went to work on weekends at a pizza shop. I was the short order cook. I cooked the fries, onion rings, clams, fried chicken and hamburgers. I ate for free, and I love to eat. I especially liked the beer battered onion rings cooked to a perfect golden brown. I nibbled whenever I had cooked someone a good batch, as long as the boss wasn't looking. I didn't like to work but I needed the cash for my junk food and cigarette habits. I also had money to buy fireworks. I remember one time my two friends and I were in the woods and I had a bunch of fireworks. We started a small fire from leaves and I'd throw in a few firecrackers. The firecrackers would blow out the fire. Thinking this was pretty interesting, we all agreed to make a large fire and throw in a pack of firecrackers. We did, and instead of blowing the fire out, it blew the fire all over the place. Now trees were burning and houses weren't far off. One of my friends was trapped between a large boulder and the fire. I tried putting the fire out with my new school jacket; it only made things worse. I never liked that jacket anyway.

Panicking, I ran to my house and screamed for my father to call the fire department. I was rushing to fill buckets with water when I looked up to notice my sister's girl friend trying to get my attention. This girl was always trying to get my attention. She would always come over to me while she was visiting my older sister. She always wanted me to let her sit on my lap or visa versa. I was a little naive and missed out on something that could have been interesting. But she always made me feel uncomfortable as I saw she was a chaser; besides, she had a nose like Pinocchio. As I was trying to hurry and get the water to put out the fire, she was lifting up her skirt wanting me to comment on her new garters, nylons and panties. I had to stop and at least take a look. All this was happening as the fire raged on in the woods. I will admit it was a nice view; she had a real nice figure and she did have great legs. The fire she was putting in me almost swayed me to forget about putting out the fire in the woods, but it just wasn't the right time. I think I must have grown up a little because for the first time I can recall I wasn't just thinking of me. I just shook my head in disbelief at my older sister's girl friend and ran away with the water. The fire department was not far away and they responded quickly. Thank God they got it all out before it did any damage to anyone or anyone's home. Of course my father was furious. He took all of the remaining fireworks and put them down the garbage disposal of all places. I never got another opportunity to explore with my sister's friend either.

Life on the Streets

Chapter 7

There were the occasional juvenile experiments with drugs and alcohol. I will admit that there was also the occasional sale of the same. Getting liquor or drugs was easy if you wanted them. There was always a street drunk hanging around the liquor store willing to buy you whatever you wanted if you would pay for the guy's rot gut. We all started experimenting with alcohol at about 14 or 15 years of age. It was summer time and my parents had gone out for the day. About 6 of us met at my house. I have this one friend that I love dearly. We eventually nicknamed him T-Bird, or Bird for short. This was due to his eventual acquired taste for Thunderbird wine. We could talk Bird into most anything. I even remember the time a few of us kids wanted to try out my new BB rifle. We talked Bird into being a living target for us. We put a heavy coat on him, heavy gloves and a football helmet. We promised not to shoot him in the face, but we did not promise that we wouldn't shoot him in the legs. He was really mad at us when we kept shooting him in the legs!

    The day we were going to experiment with the alcohol Bird was with us. We knew Bird's parents were also out of town for the day and this would be a great time to see what happened when we got someone totally drunk. My dad didn't drink, but my mom would have an occasional glass of wine or anisette. My parents did have a fairly decent supply of various liqueurs around for guests and parties. I knew they wouldn't miss anything if we just had a few sips of everything in the cabinet and then filled the bottles back up with water. Bird agreed to be the test subject. I gave him a mix of everything and anything. I gave him about 4 shots of various liquors and then we waited for a reaction. Bird said he hadn't notice anything different. So I gave him another 4 shots. He downed one after another within no time, but still nothing happened! So, I hit him with another 4 shots. He had now downed about 12 shots in less than two minutes.

Then, when I least expected it, my Grandfather Pete showed up at the back door. He never knocked; he always just walked in. We were all in the kitchen as I turned around to greet Pete. I figured I was really in for it this time. I tried fast talking and told Pete my parents were away for the day visiting with my aunt. He saw all of us in the kitchen and just kept shaking his head up and down. I was hoping that he did not see the liquor, but before I could say anything else to him, "Bam," Bird just passes out on the floor. We all just stopped and looked down at Bird. Then I quickly looked back up at my Grandfather Pete in shock and amazement. He looked me in the eyes then turned around and walked home. I knew I was in big trouble for all of this.

Bird was out cold lying on the kitchen floor. All of us tried to get Bird up. He was still alive but he was totally drunk. He was still drunk even after a few hours had passed by. We all agreed that we had to get him out of my house before my parents came home. We knew we had to get him sober or we would all be found out for sure. We all agreed to get him to the old army base where we could get the rest of the kids to help us get him sober. Then we all walked as a group with Bird held up between us until we got to the camp. We sent out one of the guys to get the rest of the gang. The girls showed up with thermoses full of black coffee. Bird was puking his guts up by now and was still pretty drunk even though 4 hours had gone by. We then decided to take him to his house and stick him under a cold shower. Time was passing and soon Bird's parents would be home. We were all having a great time and Bird was really ticked off when we stripped him naked and put him in the shower. Eventually we got Bird dressed and got him into his bed. We all got out of there before his parents arrived.

The next afternoon Bird finally came around. He was mad at all of us for a long time after this incident. I eventually found out that he was angry at us because the girls saw him naked when we gave him a shower. I tried to tell him that this was a good thing as the girls would probably want him more! He didn't buy it. As for me, I thought my life would be cut short after this incident got to my parents via Pete. I was trying to figure out my defense strategy. I even thought that maybe I should just come clean and beg for mercy. I decided against coming clean and instead decided to wait it out. It was the right move because I waited and nothing happened. Pete never said a word to my parents or to me. Now, that's a "great" grandfather!

Every so often there was a weekend "rumble" with a rival gang. I remember one night when two of my friends and I were just hanging out on the corner. A station wagon with five guys from another gang pulled up. We were 15 years old and they were 17 years old. I knew a few of these kids. I also knew these kids were looking for trouble, and they were not going home without causing some. There was this one kid with them whose father was the police lieutenant at the local station. This kid was a real loser and to say that I didn't care for him at all is being very polite.

The kid who I couldn't stand hung out the window of the car and started mouthing off something about one of us little punks saying something about his mother. I think he was trying to impress the other kids that were in the car with him. I was always a wise guy and wasn't about to be intimidated by this jerk or anyone else. I spoke up and said "I know it couldn't have been me, I really like your mother. In fact, no other woman can give me the action that she can! I knew saying this would cause this kid to make a move so that he could save face in front of the other kids. My motto has always been "just shut up and go for it." As he was halfway out of the door of the car I slammed the door shut on him and whacked him as hard as I could. I then turned to see my two "friends" running away. They were lovers, not fighters.

All of the bad boys were now out of the car. I was all alone and I knew I was in for it. I did get in a few good swings before they managed to get my coat up over my head so that I couldn't swing at them anymore. Then they smashed something against the side of my head and out I went. It felt like I was hit with a brick. The next thing I remember I woke up in the gutter. My head was killing me and I was seeing triple of everything. I don't know how long I was lying there. I had a serious concussion. I eventually managed to get home and went to bed only to vomit all night. Being a dumb 15 years old, I did not know anything about concussions. I never wanted my family to make anything out of the incident, figuring I would eventually deal with those kids on my own. Having trouble with this kid whose father was the police lieutenant was a problem. The cops came around too much already.

About a month later, four of the guys and I were hanging out on the streets. It was a very cold winter night. Then this brand new Cadillac pulled up to us. The kid I didn't care for was driving the Cadillac, and this time he was alone. I wanted a big piece of him! He saw me and pulled the car up out of my reach. He got out of the car and said he just wanted to apologize. I told him where he could stick his apology. He kept insisting and inviting all the guys to get in the car and get out of the cold. It was cold and they all wanted to get in. I refused and they all prodded me until I gave in. I figured I would get even with this guy at another time. Then this kid took all of us for a little ride.

Before we knew it this kid was hitting 60 miles an hour on tiny side roads meant for 20 miles an hour. He then went flying up this hill. We all knew there was a stop sign on the other side of the hill. We all started yelling at him to just stop the car and let us out. But it was too late. There, stopped at the stop sign, was another car. The idiot just slammed into the other car and pushed it through the intersection into a big old oak tree. Then the idiot jumps out of the driver's seat and starts laughing as he is running away from the wrecked cars. The driver of the other car that he hit took off after him. The idiot shouted something back to us but only one of the guys heard what he was saying. My friend Goose was in the front seat and he heard what the idiot was saying. We nicknamed my friend Goose because of the way he walked. Goose was on probation and couldn't afford any more problems. Goose jumped out of the car and told us all to get out and run because the Cadillac was stolen. I was in the back seat with Squirrel and Bird. (We nicknamed my friend Squirrel because he was nuts.) Squirrel and I jumped out the windows as Bird was still in the car trying to open his door.

We just stood outside the car door looking at him and wondering what he was doing. The door was obviously broken. So we both screamed at him, "Bird, just jump over the seat! We have to get out of here, the cops are coming!" He finally came to his senses and got out of the car. We started running in the opposite direction from everyone else. As we went past the car we hit I noticed that a lady and a little kid were in the car. They both looked okay, but we couldn't stick around to be sure. The lady started screaming at us and I can't say that I didn't blame her. I actually felt like a total jerk!

We ran as fast as we could and made it to Bird's cellar. Bird's cellar was sort of a hang out place for us. We played pool and cards. A bunch of the guys were there and we told them what happened. We were all excited and we all thought we were lucky to get away. Bird and Squirrel started playing pool and me and few of the guys started a game of poker. About an hour had past and there was a knock on the door. "Hey! Open up, it's me Goose!" At first we were relieved because he had gotten away. But this was short lived, as he came in with two of Boston's finest detectives right behind him. They had all of us. The only one they didn't have was the idiot.

Bird had to go get his father, and his father wasn't very happy. There was a lot a screaming and bad language. Eventually the detectives brought us upstairs one at a time for a little conversation. I was last. When I got upstairs Bird was vomiting in a bucket. Our stories of what happened all matched. The cops said they really wanted Idiot and not us. They said no one was seriously hurt; if we all agreed to tell our story in court the cops would not charge us with anything. Having more than enough of Idiot, I had no problem agreeing. Of course, they couldn't just let us all go home on our own; they would need to escort us.

They dropped Goose and Squirrel off first. They had already talked to Goose's parents so that was no big deal. Squirrel's parents were older, having this late in life child. His parents forced him to become an altar boy, that was a joke in itself. When the detective told Squirrel's mom what happened she fainted right there in the doorway. It was finally my turn to be taken home, but the cops weren't taking me straight home. They wanted to drive by Idiot's house to see if he had shown up. He had shown up but then he went out again. His mother informed the detectives that he had also stolen his father's gun. Great! Now Idiot is out there armed and dangerous. We stopped by a local bar room where the bikers hung out. Idiot would sometimes hang out there.

He wasn't there, thank God, and it was getting late so the cops decided to take me home. I told them that since it was now close to 2:00 AM my parents would probably be asleep. Maybe they could call my parents tomorrow and give me a little time to explain things to them. They could just let me go in the house. "Nice try kid," they said.

I knew this wasn't going to be fun. The detectives waited inside the front door. My parents were both sleeping and I knocked on their bedroom door. My mother answered and started in on me, "Don't you know how late it is!" She started screaming little nasty Italian words I won't repeat. I asked her to calm down. I then told her that I needed her and dad to come meet someone. "Now what did you do!" my mother said still screaming, "Bobby, Bobby, wake up the son of _____ did something!" My mother is purebred Italian all right. She's only 4'8" and probably weighs all of about 100 lbs. soaking wet. But my mom is full of the Italian fire when she's mad. She or any of her brothers would take on a giant without a second thought and, my money would be on my mom or her brothers.

As soon as the cops told her what happened, she started in on me again. I was too big for her to hit. Hitting me hurt her more than it did me, so instead she would bite, or grab a bunch of my skin and pinch really hard. Then again sometimes she got a hold of my ear. She did whatever was necessary to express her feelings. She went for all three this time and I can still feel it, "OOOW! Ma, Ma, OOOW! Okay, Okay, Ma you win, you win, I'll be good, I'll be good!" There she went, right in front of the cops. Oh, the cops thought it was hilarious! The cops finally left and I got my parents to calm down and go back to bed.

Later the cops finally caught Idiot. All my friends and I had to show up in court but we did not have to testify. Idiot's father had a lot of clout and had most of the charges dropped. Idiot had to pay the damages and perform a four year hitch in the Navy. At least Idiot was now out of my life.

My Aggy

Chapter 8

There were also the occasions when one of the guys might "borrow" something without the permission of the owner. We considered it borrowing, as the owner would eventually get their property back or the insurance money to pay for it. Returned property would most likely be missing some parts and most likely be torched. Like I said, we were not angels. None of us were thinking about the owners feelings. Sometimes we would just take cars and go on joy rides. Sometimes we would just crash a car into something to see what happened. It was an incident like this when I first laid eyes on "My Ag."

I was fifteen and the guys had "borrowed" somebody's car. We had taken it up to the old abandoned army base to take off all the saleable items. I was perched up at a lookout spot in case any unwanted law enforcement might pay us a visit. My friends had now gotten the car to the point where they were ready to do the science experiment. The experiment involved covering the car in gasoline, putting a gasoline soaked rag into the gas tank of the stripped car, then striking a match, lighting up the rag and watching what happened.

Before the guys had gotten to this point I happened to spot this new girl on the street below walking a poodle. She immediately caught my eye! She looked like Cher Bono with her straight hair. She had on a halter top, a tight pair of jeans and saddle shoes. She looked real good to me! I yelled down to her telling her to come closer. To my amazement, she did. I then made a very off colored comment on what she did for me, as well as what I wanted to do to her! She didn't get startled and run off screaming as most of the other girls did. Instead, she looked me in the eye, smiled, then started waving her middle finger at me! She then turned around and slowly walked away. That did it for me! Call me easy, but this girl was hot and I wanted her. I had never seen her before. I knew everyone in the neighborhood and they all knew me as one of the "bad" boys. This girl must have known that, but she was not intimidated.

A few days later I was over my cousins shooting some "hoop" with some of the guys. This was the next time I saw her. There was this kid that hung around us from time to time. He had a short leg from polio and he was a real wise guy. Most of us didn't care for him. This kid eventually grew up to be a major heroin dealer. He's probably dead by now. Anyway, he had this special bike that he got around on. It had a special block peddle so he could ride it with his bad leg. This girl must have seen me playing with the guys and she figured she would get my attention if she stole this kid's bike. Normally I wouldn't have cared less, but she was special. So I had to play the hero supposedly for the kid's sake. I chased after her. She didn't try very hard to get away. I caught up to her and told her she had to give me her number. She told me to get lost. So I said okay, at least give me your name.

"Why should I?" she said.

I said, "Cause I think your hot and want you to go out with me!"

Then she said, "The names Ag and where would you take me out to?"

I said, "Where ever you want to go, darling." I didn't get her number but I did get the date. I met her at the Oriental theatre the next Saturday. The movie playing was "The Fly." I don't remember seeing much of the movie. My attention was on Ag! We were both only fifteen but I knew then like I'd know 38 years later, I was falling in love and she was my soul mate.

After that day we were inseparable. We were like George and Gracie Allen, Ricky and Lucy Arnez, Fred and Alice Cramden, The Lone Ranger and Tonto and then don't forget Adam and Eve.

Ag told me that she was a pure bred Albanian and she was proud of it. I just wondered what an Albanian was. I thought she meant she was into to some weird kind of religion or something. She then told me Albania is a country. I'd never heard about any country named Albania. Finally she showed it to me on a map. Then I said, "Oh, so it's part of Greece!" That's a bad thing to say to an Albanian! I told her I was an American. Then she pressed me about it so I told her I was a mutt, a mongrel, you know, a Heinz 57. She still seemed a bit out there, not following my meaning, so I told her; I'm a mixed breed but I am mainly Italian and proud of it. I may not be a purebred, but as I hear it, Italy conquered Albania along with the rest of the known world! She's wild when she gets mad! I don't know why, but I love it when she gets mad!

Ag is the youngest of three. Her sister is the oldest and then comes her brother. Her father and mother ran a Mom and Pops variety store in South Boston for a while. Ag grew up mostly in South Boston, or "Southie" as we call it. Her family, aunts, uncles and cousins all traveled in a group. They all watched out for each other and they all kept Ag on a short leash. She wasn't allowed much freedom and wasn't allowed to go out at night. This was okay with me because I could hang out with the other kids. We had to keep our love affair a secret from her family for a long time and made good use of the old army camp. Her family would not approve of Ag going out with anyone who wasn't an Albanian. When her family traveled it was always together. You usually saw at least three "Caddy's" driving by the corner where we hung out. It was like the Albanian mob. Ag was always in the back seat straining to see me as she past by. Being with Ag kept me out of more trouble that I would have probably managed to get into with the guys.

Employment

Chapter 9

When I was about 16 years old I went to work as a bus boy at a fancy restaurant. This was a good thing, especially when I helped my friend Tommy get a job working with me. Tommy was sixteen and had his drivers license. At the restaurant there was this hostess who looked like a call girl. She was a witch with a "b." She didn't care for me or Tommy because I caught her fooling around with the boss. The boss was married and the boss's wife also didn't care for the witch. The witch figured I told Tommy about her and the boss. The witch thought Tommy and I might tell the boss's wife more than what the wife was already was suspicious of. The witch had a good thing going with the boss. She had a fur coat, a nice car and a lot of fancy jewelry. We all knew she couldn't get that stuff on a hostess's salary. You name it and the witch had it. We all knew that "all her flash" was all compliments of the boss.

She didn't have to work very hard, as a hostess I mean. You could plainly see she liked things just the way they were. She wanted to get rid of Tommy and me to keep things a secret. She wasn't too bright as I never would have said anything anyway because then the boss would have fired me or Tommy long before he would fire her. The way I saw things what's the big deal anyway? The head chef was fooling around with all the waitresses. He was also married and was not discrete. He could care less who knew. Most of the waitresses were also married and fooling around with the customers. I never would have said anything about the head chef. He always made sure I got a hefty sliced prime rib sandwich when I would come in to work. He then would top my meal off with those puffs filled with coffee ice cream, covered in hot fudge and smothered under whipped cream. This guy knew the way to my heart! He could do no wrong in my eyes.

We had been working there for several months, and except for the guy who ran the dish washer, Tommy and I were usually the last ones to leave. We never paid much attention to the dish washer. He couldn't speak English very well so we thought he couldn't squeal on us. One night the bartender gave Tommy the keys to the beer locker, telling him to bring up a few cases of beer to the bar. We both figured this was going to be pay dirt! Tommy got a hold of me immediately. To us, we figured this guy had handed us the keys to Fort Knox. We ran to the beer locker. There were cases and cases of beer! Quickly, we both grabbed a couple of cases and hid them in another storage room. We figured they would never miss four cases of beer when they had so many. We also figured we could get them when we left that night, as Tommy had his sister's car. Finally, everyone left except for the dish washer. Tommy backed the car up to the rear door. We picked up the beer and put it in the car, then drove back to the corner where we hung around and stashed the beer in a safe place. We were flying high. The guys would pay top dollar for this beer and we could get wasted for free!

Well anyway, to our great surprise, they either counted the cases of beer, or the dishwasher squealed. The witch called us both up the next day to inform us that our services were no longer required at their fine establishment. It was no big deal to me, but it really mattered to my mom. She flipped out on me. She was screaming at me, but at least she wasn't pulling my ears, pinching me or biting me. She was screaming a lot of nasty Italian words at me along with, "What did you do! You had to have done something! I know you did something!"

I had to defend myself or she wouldn't stop. She works

herself up. So I said, "Ma, Ma, come on, would your baby boy do anything wrong? It was the witch Ma, she's been fooling around with the boss and I caught her. That's what this is all about!"

Then she started chanting "boota, boota, butana!" She was calling the witch a whore in Italian and at least the heat was off me. Of course I wasn't going to say anything about the beer!

It wasn't long after this that I got a job working at the first KFC opening up in our area. They taught me to cook the chicken. I cooked some mean chicken, just right! One of the benefits of working there was you could have all the chicken you could eat. You couldn't bring it home, you had to eat it there and you had to pay for anything else you wanted. That was fine with me! I would put down a dozen chicken legs a night. It also had other benefits—girls! Every time the boss was on the phone we got the chance to make the moves on the girls. It was a little bit of both of the things that made me happy.

School

Chapter 10

Time went on. I did not care for school much. I had a hard time just staying awake in school out of pure boredom. I often wondered if the any of the things they taught me in school would be of any use to me in the real world. You learn a lot more growing up on the streets. Innocence flies away by age 10. You get to know all the games and all the players. I would skip school without much prodding from any of my buddies. Most of the time, I was with Bird. We would take the train in town and do a little shoplifting or go to "Filenes" basement and hideout under the clothes racks. From that vantage point, we would watch the unsuspecting women while they were changing, trying out clothes, not realizing we were there. I know, we were juvenile perverts looking to fill our curiosity. Sometimes we would "party" down by the tracks, or up at the old army base, or party in someone's house while the people went out to work all day. Once, I skipped school for at least two weeks straight.

I had my father's signature down to a "T." I would send notes to the school on how I had broken my leg, was being tutored at home and was getting along fine. I would check the mail and dispose of any letter coming from my school. I missed the mail one day and didn't know they had sent home a notice for my parents to come in to meet with my teachers. They all knew my father, as he taught in the Boston school system and he was considered one of their own. Well, I was found out. I don't think I can ever recall my father being so mad. My punishment was to strip wallpaper and paint for a month. When I went back to school the teachers treated me like I was "Americas Most Wanted." The teachers' comments to me: "Oh, how could I do such a despicable act, had I no shame! How could I ever do such a thing, especially to my father?"

They weren't going to expel me or even suspend me, but my father insisted that I at least be suspended. Like that was a bad thing! A little over a month had past and I figured it was all behind me. It was now late spring. It was a beautiful day! It was much too nice of a day to waste in school! Bird was prodding me and I said to myself, Oh what the hell! I skipped again. We spent the day in town. Then we made sure we were back around the school just as it was getting out. I figured there was no way the teachers would believe I skipped again, not after all I just went through! But to my surprise they had called my parents! Of course, it had to be my older sister who found me when school had gotten out. She just relished telling me how much trouble I was in. At least I knew what to expect when I got home. This time my mother kept insisting it was "that girl's" fault, meaning Ag. But Ag had nothing to do with it. They called Ag's parents ranting and raving how she was to stay away from their son. They forbid me to make any contact with her. Of course I could care less what my parents wanted. The "no contact" with Ag only lasted 15 minutes. I had another phone my parents didn't know about and would plug it into the phone jack in my sister's room. Then I would sneak out and meet with her whenever I could. It took a long time and a lot of sneaking around for the whole thing to blow over.

The Wheels

Chapter 11

All of the kids I hung around would get around via public transportation before we all got our drivers licenses. When we all finally got our drivers licenses, we all got the cars! Chrysler, Ford and Chevy, American made, that's all that mattered. Life was a blast. If it felt good, then go for it! My first car was a '61 Chevy Impala SS Convertible. It was white with baby blue interior.

I remember one time when I had to fix the muffler on my car. The car was up on blocks and I just needed one more clamp to finish. My father had recently bought this Oldsmobile Delta 88. It was the first new car, as opposed to a used car, that he had ever bought. He really liked that car. He only had the car for two days, and since my car was up on blocks I asked him if I could just use his car to run to the store to buy a muffler clamp. He was reluctant at first, but then gave me the keys to his new car. I drove to store, locked up his car and ran in and out of the store in under 2 minutes. I walked over to where I had parked the car, but there was no car! I thought maybe I must have parked it somewhere else. I searched the whole parking lot, but found no car! Woo! I knew this was going to be very bad!

I ran back into the store and found a cop on duty. I told him that my father's brand new car was stolen! The cop said, "When did your father buy the car?"

I said, "Two days ago."

The cop then said, "Well then, now it's a used car!"

The store manager let me use the phone to call my father. When my father answered the phone I tried to tell him what happened as gently as possible. At first he would not believe me and kept telling me to knock it off and get home. I finally had to put the cop on the phone. When the cop was done talking to my father he handed me the phone. I kept the earpiece a good distance away from my ear as not to hurt my ear drum with the words that followed to me from my father. The cop did give me a ride home. I just wasn't sure I wanted to go there. I did go back outside to finish fixing my car and to get away from my father's ranting and raving.

They found my father's car a few weeks later. It was smashed up and the police told my father it was used in a hold up. My father told me that the insurance company considered the car used, even though he only had the car a few days. He constantly reminds me of how much money he lost; again with his disapproval thing.

I soon graduated from high school and bought a 1965 T-bird. Many a night Ag and I would fog up the windows of that car. Ag had a 1965 Mustang. When she drove, she was a wild woman; forget about red lights and stop signs. Ag would fly right through. She was Mustang Sally! The kids I hung around all had "muscle" cars. There were 57 Chevy's, a couple of Corvette's, a couple of Z 28 Camaro's and even a Ford Cobra Mustang. All of the kids I hung around had nice cars, everyone except Bird. While all of us had wild cars, Bird had a 62 Chevy Bel Air, six cylinders, four doors.

I remember one time that Bird's brother Billy had gone to a fraternity party at Stonehill College. Billy was gone all night and never made it back home. Billy called Bird the next morning and asked Bird to come and get him. Billy had to get back home before his parents found out where he was and that he hadn't come home. It was early on a Sunday morning. Bird had called up a few of the guys to see if they would go with him for the ride. I was one of them. Sometimes Bird was like a little old man, especially when it came to driving. He always stayed within the speed limit and he never knew where he was going.

We drove down a country road; there was no traffic and no people around. It seemed like something out of a ghost story. Two of the guys rode up front with Bird while Jason and I rode in the back. We were driving beside this long stone wall that enclosed a large field. Jason and I saw this horse running though the field at a full gallop. The horse had a saddle on it but there was no rider in sight. The horse seemed to be heading in the direction of the stone wall. The more we watched, the more we could see that we were headed in a collision course with the horse. We figured the horse couldn't get past the wall. Bird slowed the car to a stop. Then in an instant the horse turned and jumped the wall. The horse landed right smack on the hood of Bird's car. First the BAM, as the horse came crashing down on the hood of Bird's car. Then another BAM, as the front tires blew out. Then SMASH! The horse's head hit the front windshield! When windshield glass first shatters it breaks up in such a way that you can't see through it. Within 5 seconds after this happened there was another big SMASH! This time the glass exploded everywhere and the horse's head was through the windshield thrashing wildly, as its head was stuck.

Blood was going every where while the horse was whipping its head around trying to get free. The guys in the front seat were freaking out. They were all screaming and covered in blood. Get this thing off of us! Get it off! Get it off! Jay and I jumped out of the back seat just as the horse seemed to calm down and then the horse just slid off the hood of the car. The horse lay motionless for a few seconds on the ground. We thought it was dead. Then all of sudden the horse woke up, struggled to its feet and just trotted away down the road. We could clearly see that the horse's neck was broken by the way it was moving and how its head was tilted to almost a 45 degree angle.

We were all outside of the car now. The car was totaled

and sitting in the middle of the road. The front tires were flat and there was no one around. Who was ever going to believe this? We all started roaring in laughter, all of us except for Bird. He wasn't very happy. While we were still laughing we all heard this moaning coming from the other side of the wall. We turned at this point to see this guy all disheveled in full riding gear standing up behind the wall. There was a rider on the horse! We all just were roaring with more laughter at this bizarre happening. They had to tow Bird's car home. When we arrived at Bird's house, Bird's brother was already there. He had gotten a ride from one of the girls at the school after he got tired of waiting for us to pick him up. The only good thing that did happen was Bird's Bel Air was totaled and his next car was an Olds 442.

Beyond the Call of Duty

Chapter 12

Time was going by and it was now 1968. Up to this point I was living an "if it feels good go for it" self-centered life. The Vietnam War was still on going and so was the draft. I was 17 years old and I had just graduated from high school. I was happy and free back then with no real worries or concerns. I was dating my young teen sweetheart Ag, who later became, and still is, my wife. It was coming up to my 18th birthday and a lottery system was developed to pick out who was to be drafted. The lottery consisted of numbers that corresponded to your birth date that were randomly selected. I had a low draft number due to my birth date and I was scheduled to be drafted. Most likely I would have been sent to Vietnam.

    My father signed me up in the Naval Air Force, thinking it would minimize my chances of being killed in the war. I wasn't going to college nor was I seeking any deferment. I was in good shape. I do believe in my country and I am no coward. Perhaps I could have tried to dodged the draft like a lot of guys did, but I strongly felt and still feel that is a coward's way of handling ones duty. Maybe I was maturing, but I wasn't just centered on me this time. People were dying in Vietnam. Guys I knew. If everyone ran away, were would this country be? I had no intentions of a military career. I did not agree with the United States' involvement in Vietnam. Nor did I have any desire to have any part of the war. But I still felt that I was obligated to serve my country. When I joined the military I was expecting to experience what I believed was something that turned boys into men. What I experienced showed me the worst of a world that I did not know existed at the time.

I started my entry into the service being sent to boot camp in Millington, Tennessee. In boot camp I witnessed various abusive situations. I never thought this kind of thing was allowed to happen. I saw men being hit with rifle butts by Marine drill sergeants. I saw a man being forced to sleep under a barracks wearing only his under shorts in cold inclement weather. I saw men forced to enter and stay in a mud pool filled with leaches all night. I saw a man forced to run with concrete blocks tied to his ankles. I saw a man forced to shave with a bucket over his head while running. One day we were taken to the swimming pool and lined up on one side of the pool. Several men who did not know how to swim were lined up across from us on the other side of the pool. We were ordered to stand at attention and not to move while the men who could not swim were thrown into the pool. The drill sergeants taunted the non-swimmers, as they struggled in the water. One man eventually drowned, but was resuscitated. Sink or swim. It just did not sit right with me. I thought it was all cruel and wrong. Looking back on it, I suppose the sergeants were doing what they had to do. If you couldn't learn here, being on a ship or plane that goes down, or in any tough situation, could mean certain death. Not following orders could also be hazardous to your health, or hazardous to others with you.

Boot camp was brainwashing and I learned to keep my mouth shut, do whatever, whenever, and however I was told. In boot camp I was taught and brainwashed to believe that I was no longer an individual; I was no longer a person, but the property of the United States Government. I was government property that my superiors could do with what they wanted to. I learned there was no quitting or running away. The least a deserter would receive would be a dishonorable discharge that would stay with them, ruining their entire life. As this was during a time when America was at war, I also learned that deserters could face imprisonment or even execution. I was also taught to hate and given the desire to kill.

After boot camp I was sent to a military "A" school in Pensacola, Florida. I was trained to be a photographer. After "A" school I was sent to Newport, RI to await orders for active duty. A Lt. Colonel told me that I would most likely be assigned to a river boat squadron doing scouting and reconnaissance in Vietnam. I clearly understood that being a scout was not a good thing and I could very likely be killed. Naturally, I was not very happy to hear this news. He then said that there was a possible alternative to this duty. He said that there was another special squadron that needed a photo mate. They operated out of Rhode Island and would occasionally have duty in Iceland. He said that I would have to volunteer for this squadron. I could not understand why I had to volunteer, as this sounded to good to be true. Remembering my geography, I remembered that Iceland had the girls and Greenland had the ice. Being a red-blooded teenage male I guess I was thinking with the wrong brain. I thought this had to be a better alternative than the river boats in Vietnam. As I was a naive 18-year-old, I agreed and signed. I was sent to Quonset Point, RI to join this squadron. Well it wasn't Iceland, but an "ICE" land that the squadron went to; Antarctica, to be exact. It was called "Operation Deep Freeze, Squadron VXE-6." I was tricked and stuck. From this point on I learned that you never trust and never volunteer.

My first experience with what even the Quonset Point Base called the "Animal Squadron" was to learn first hand what it felt like to be brutally beaten and raped. When I reported for duty, I was told by the officer in charge that I had to go and report to the barracks officer and stow my gear. I was then told by the barracks officer to go into the barracks area and pick out a bunk. It was an area with bunk beds and metal lockers. The area was partitioned in cubed sections of four to seven bunk beds enclosed inside metal lockers. Entrance into a cube was via one 3-foot wide space between two lockers. When I went into one of the cubes to pick out an empty bunk and a locker I noted there were about a half dozen men in the cube. They were not very friendly and most of them were a lot bigger than me. I had my Navy white uniform on at the time. I could feel that I was not accepted and then one of the men started to talk to me. He said, "You're a new guy, right?"

I said, "Yes," and told him my name.

He didn't tell me his but just asked me if I was a member of the "Turtle Club."

I had never heard of the Turtle Club so I asked, "What is the Turtle Club?"

He then said, "Wrong answer." In the same moment he punched me so hard in the stomach that it knocked the wind out of me. As I bent over in both pain and in an attempt to catch my breath, men seemed to come out of the woodwork. They encircled me and blocked the entrance of the cube. There were at least 12 to 15 men, maybe more. Before I was able to catch my breath they all pounced on me, and proceeded to beat me and kick me. I tried to fight them off but there were too many of them. They held me up and while they were beating me they removed my pants and bent me over. The guy that asked if I was a member of the turtle club was screaming all sorts of insults (put in a nice way) at me and telling me to go ahead and keep on screaming, no one would come to help me, and no one did. Then this guy started to talk some men that were behind me and told them to "present arms." At first I thought these guys were biting my rectum because I felt this awful sharp pain, as I felt my flesh being penetrated and ripped. In fact that's all I tried to convince myself had happened for years. I could not actually see what was going on or exactly see who was violating me as they were behind me. I was being held in a bent over position. My only view was in front of me and looking down at the blood as it ran down my legs. I was being raped. I kept going in and out of shock. I remember looking up, seeing them all laughing and cheering on the men behind me. It seemed like hours when eventually I heard someone say, "That's enough blood." Then they let me go and I fell to the ground. I don't even remember how I got up and got dressed. One of them told me not to tell anybody of what just happened as it would be my word against theirs and there were more of them. He said that I must understand that "no one" saw anything and "no report" would be filed. Then he said to me, "If anyone asks me from now on if I am a member of the turtle club, I tell them "You bet your sweet ass I am" and now I know why.

 I was just a boy and they had just destroyed my life and turned me into a person full of rage, distrust, unmerited quilt, undeserving shame, and forever filled with a monster named Post Traumatic Stress Disorder (PTSD). This was way beyond an involuntary hazing initiation. This was a crime; a crime that the military ignored whenever I tried to report it. I believe but I cannot say for sure that some of the men, or rather "animals," that assaulted me had just returned from a "winter" tour of duty on Antarctica. I believe these "animals" that had wintered over in Antarctica initiated this event. A tour, summer or winter, lasted between 5 to 7 months. These "animals" had been pent up in a very isolated situation. During the winter months the sun does not shine in Antarctica. It gets beyond cold and outside travel is extremely limited. These animals had a lot of pent up feelings and energy. It was as though I was a piece of raw meat being fed to a den of lions. All I wanted to do was to run as far away from there as I could and never look back.

 I don't remember how I got to the bus station, but I do remember the bus ride home. Even today some of the details of the trauma are still blotted from my mind. My white pants were covered in blood. I tied a jacket around my waste to cover my backside. I remember that I couldn't sit down and how much pain I was in. I didn't know what I was going to do. I didn't want to go back there. I was only 18 years old. I thought of running away to Canada. I couldn't speak French and how would I survive? I couldn't tell anyone. No one would ever believe it. This sort of thing doesn't happen to "guys," it's too unimaginable. I couldn't tell my parents, they would be disgusted and ashamed of me. I couldn't go to my family doctor, as he would surely tell my parents. I couldn't tell my friends they would think I was a homosexual or just simply not have anything to do with me. I couldn't tell my girlfriend exactly what happened or she would surely leave me. If I ran away I would be a deserter, they would probably catch me, bring me back and I would probably be sent to jail or executed. I just didn't know what to do.

I remember when I finally reached my house no one was home. I was relieved and quickly ran to take a shower. I then stuck toilet tissue on my rectum. I put my clothes in a paper bag, threw them in the trash outside and got out of the house before anyone got home. I knew I would have to face my girlfriend. She would see the cuts, black and blues, but nothing else. I told her partly what happened, but left out the rape as I knew she couldn't accept it. She was furious just over the beating. If she only knew the whole story I was certain she would not have stayed with me.

Though I didn't want to go back, there was no other choice. I had to bury this thing, go back, and go on. I found it was a mistake reporting the incident to my immediate supervisors. It made every thing worse. They did not look at this incident as a crime. This was an accepted practice. They all knew the story. "Ass packing," as it was called, was a commonplace event with this squadron! There is no "nice way" to say this. The victim's anus cavity would be filled with a variety of things. It did not matter what was shoved into the anus cavity as long as something was shoved into the victim's anus cavity. In a sick way they felt this was what made you a man, made you one of them, a form of acceptance. Just suck it up! No investigation of my reporting the complaint was ever made! My superiors did not consider an investigation warranted. The perpetrators were not looked at by the military as if they did something wrong. The perpetrators were not about to come forward and state they did anything wrong either. Turtle Club membership was a non-voluntary Navy tradition for anyone that traveled below the south 30 degree parallel. It was considered by the military hierarchy as part of an acceptance in belonging to the Navy. The commonplace "hazing" as I have learned still happens today and is carried out in various ways.

The Ice

Chapter 13

Well if assault and rape were not bad enough, I was soon to find out it was going to get worse. I ended up doing two tours on Antarctica, commonly known as "The Ice." I was not supposed to go on the second tour and was basically kidnapped. The second tour was explained to me by my immediate superiors, "to prove a point." The point was that I was the "property" of the U.S. Government and not an individual. Any "story telling" would be viewed as an act of treason, not in the best interest of the United States. I was shown this so that it was perfectly clear to me. They proved to me that they had all the power. They owned me and could do anything they wanted with me. It was just like in the barracks: go ahead scream, no one will come to help you.

Antarctica is the best prison in the world. It is isolated from the rest of the world's eyes. At first it seemed so beautiful, but in living there I got to see past its beauty. There are no bars needed, as there is no way to escape. There is no vegetation; just cold, "real cold," snow, ice, volcanoes and lava rock. It always reminded me of death. It is a very hostile environment. The closest example to explain the experience of living on the ice would be to imagine living on the moon. I prayed every day that I would get back to the world. I felt abandoned on the ice. Even though there were other men there with me, I felt so very alone. The government held the only keys and they were the only way I could get back to the world. I was forced to trust the same people that violated me. I had to live, eat and sleep with my perpetrators day in and day out. I either skipped meals or ate at the photo lab as much as possible. I remember every time that I went to the chow hall I would always look at whoever came in and wonder if they were one of the "animals" that raped me. When I did go to the chow hall I would go there real early, or real late, whenever the least amount of people would be there. I found this duty to be a prisoner of war sentence, with my own fellow soldiers as the guards. It was a prison sentence for doing my duty in trying to serve my country.

I felt like a kidnapped prisoner forced to perform slave labor. I slept in my clothes and didn't sleep much in the hut. I slept mostly in the dark room in the photo lab. I was supposed to sleep in a bunk, in a Quonset hut, in a 6x9 room with no windows and only one way of escape. There was a bunk bed in the room. I slept on the top bed and the late "Late Night Show" host Johnny Carson's son, Rick, slept on the bottom bunk. Sleeping in the hut was risky. There was no noise allowed. The no noise policy had advantages as I could wake up quickly if anyone entered the hut. I could easily end up the subject of a blanket party while I was sleeping. That's why I always slept with my clothes on. I could hear the "blanket party perpetrators," as I will call them, as they entered the hut in search for the next victim. These perpetrators were a group of men who would administer "punishment." These guys would cover the victim in a blanket, beat them or do worse things to them (note what happened to me above). They would always be looking to administer an "ass packing" to an unsuspecting victim.

I personally witnessed these events a number of times. I was forced by my immediate supervisor, Chief Pudsey, to participate in one of these hazing rituals. Chief Pudsey told me that if I did not participate I would be reinitiated. The victim they chose this time was also a chief. His leg was broken during the assault on him. Various items, including cigarette butts, ashes, cherries, syrups, peanut butter, and marshmallow were shoved up his anal cavity. This was all topped off with a lit cigar shoved into his anal cavity; the lit end of the cigar was left hanging out of his rectum. This victim was also photographed. Pudsey ordered me to get into the picture. I even have some of the pictures of this incident that were given to me by Pudsey. Pudsey told me that the pictures were to be a reminder of what happened to story tellers. Pudsey also told me that the pictures could also be used to implicate me if any stories of what happens in this squadron were to get out.

It was even rumored that sometimes the blanket party perpetrators would take a victim a few miles from the base and drop them off naked after they were done with him. The victim would never make it back alive and no body would ever be found. Not with the weather and quick snowfall cover. I never witnessed this happening, but did notice that men would end up "missing." I was told that the victim must have "cracked up" and taken a walk. I never saw any search parties go out during the time period a supposed victim was last seen alive or after a victim was reported missing. But I didn't get to see everything that happened in Antarctica. Being nineteen and experiencing things first hand easily made me believe that anything was possible on the ice. I never personally experienced a blanket party done to me, nor did I enjoy even the thought of being the subject of one. On my second tour I was tipped off that I was scheduled to be the victim of a blanket party. But I firmly believe that someone was looking out for me. Ag got my father to have my grandfather Pete get in touch with his old friend Congressman Burke to see if anything could be done for me. Congressman Burke started checking things out, which got my superiors nervous. It was Congressman Burke's actions that made them release me from active duty and send me home alive.

Life in Antarctica was bad enough. On top of everything else, I had to contend with the little things that I always took for granted. I was only allowed a two-minute shower a month. I had to urinate in a funnel or in a jar. Bowel movements were done on a 3–6 man outhouse type box or in a plastic bag. The reader cannot imagine how bad it smelled, along with the no privacy factor. There were no visitors, no family, no friends, or no phone calls. There was a limited occasional phone patch allowed over a radio band. Every word spoken was monitored. A phone patch was limited to a few minutes. If I started to say something the monitors didn't like I was cut off. Mail was sparse and was also often monitored. There was no TV, no vegetation, no long walks and no women. I could get a good beating or worse by just saying "good morning" to someone. Like I said, it was "prison"!

I spent most of the time in the photo lab. I worked 12 to 14 hours a day, 7 days a week, most of which was in the darkroom that stenched of muriatic and hydrochloric acid. It was supposed to be ventilated but the fan didn't work right. However, it was somewhat safe from the human animals outside. As I stated, when I did try to report my assault to my immediate superiors it only made things worse. Whatever they could do to make life miserable for me they would gladly do it. Verbal and psychological abuse was constant. Peers could be punished for any reason your superior wanted. Punishment could be all sorts of things. Little things to serious things that could get you killed. Minor punishment would be anything from shining my superior's shoes over and over again, to private "field days" scrubbing everything and anything over and over again for no reason, to not being allowed to watch the occasional movie. Serious punishment included being set up for a blanket party, or being sent on a special "mission." Putting it mildly, a special mission could get you seriously hurt or killed. The special missions are another book in themselves.

The Damage

Chapter 14

My immediate supervisors, Warrant Officer Russell and Chief Pudsey received word in August of 1971 that I was to be released from active duty in October 1971. On October 8, 1971, personnel received the official order for my release. My records and I were in Quonset at that time. They could have just released me as ordered in Quonset Point, RI. or released me from Christchurch, New Zealand, or even released me in Antarctica. They had flights going back from all of those places. Russell and Pudsey had no intention of letting that happen. Russell and Pudsey also knew that I was getting married in February. These two men got the commanding officer (the CO) to ignore the order for my release from active duty and instead have my active duty extended. I was then sent back to the "ice" for a second tour.

When I got to the ice the second time I didn't really know if I would be coming home alive. My concern that my life was in jeopardy was substantiated, as I was placed in suspicious and dangerous situations. The first tour lasted 6 months. The second tour lasted for 4 months before the investigation started by Congressman Burke got me out of there. The CO went along with Russell and Pudsey in an attempt to cover up their disregard for my release. They fabricated this story of how an E3 nobody like me was indispensable. They sent this off to Congressman Burke in their defense of explaining why they disobeyed the Chief of Naval Operations' order and extended my active duty. The reply letter that they wrote to Congressman Burke stated that I was the only person trained to run some kind of photo equipment that I had never even heard of, never mind ever knew how to operate. I have copies of this correspondence that were sent back to me by Congressman Burke.

The CO and my immediate supervisors, hoping to stop any further investigation, had me released and put on the next flight home. Ricky Carson knew what Russell and Pudsey were doing to me. If I was released Rick would be their next victim. Rick had clout and a plan. His plan worked and he was released just before Congressman Burke's investigation had gotten me out. I tried contacting Rick later. I did not have his number and when I tried to contact him through his father, I did not get any response to my letters. Years later I heard on the news that he had died in an accident.

In a nutshell, I was beaten, raped, sodomized, humiliated, trapped, kidnapped and forced to live where my survival depended on the people who violated me. I was continually verbally, psychologically and physically abused. Then my active duty was involuntarily extended and I was forced to do a second tour in hell. All of this was done to me by the very same people that were entrusted to keep me safe. I was supposed to be one of their own.

There has been recent public awareness in the exposing of hazing and rapes. There is the scandal involving the Catholic Church. I remember a major news station ran a story about abuse in the military involving female cadets being raped. Another recent major news story told about a boy being abused in a "hazing incident." The boy, not much younger than I was at the time of my abuse, was sodomized with a banana as part of a football team hazing initiation. The boy's town and society in general seemed to have mixed opinions over the incident.

Then there was the "outcry of the atrocities" over pictures of naked Iraq prisoners being abused by our military. Only after the public saw the photographs in the press did the government react. Public sentiment can be as sick, as it is seems to be divided. Maybe incidents like this are not given enough public exposure. Some people just don't want to hear about it anymore, some people say they should have just sucked it up, and some, hopefully the majority, say this is wrong! The military wants to continue to keep this abuse under the rug. I wonder what that says about our country.

I remember growing up back in the '60's. I guess I was naive and thought behavior like this could never happen. Then again I could not believe something like this could never happen to me. People would never hear about a male being raped. Only females were raped. Then, as sick as it was, people might say that she must have asked for it! So rapes are not reported and a terrible wrong in our society is not made right. The truth gets sugar coated to make it easier to be accepted by society. Anyone that has gone through a similar situation understands that life after the rape is spent in a private "hell" most every day. The victims know all too well the permanent scarring that they carry. The thoughts and the damage done to a victim just don't go away. It only gets worse if you try to bury the memories. A victim's view of life in this world changes forever.

The military states that when you're 18 in their eyes you're a man. I have a 22-year-old son, and he's not a man, he's still a boy. I shutter to think that 18-year-old boys are given weapons and sent out to kill. Their minds are so easily molded, easily manipulated. I was only a boy, not a man. I wasn't treated like a man; I was treated like a dispensable object, an object that my superiors had no regard for. They certainly were not concerned for my safety or well-being. I'm no longer a boy and I wonder how the call to duty obligation I felt for my country was twisted into something so wrong. The military has scarred my life. I know that we must have a military force to keep our country free. With every large organization there will always be some amount of evil. The more that good people choose to do nothing about it, the more evil will flourish. In the military there is freedom of religion. You can join a cult and worship

Satan in the service. It's okay with the military. As long as you do what they want you to do, when they want you to do it.

I am still struggling with the government over my assault and the damage it has done to me, and will continue to do so. The military is all about power and force. The military polices itself. The military and its affiliate government agencies decide what wrongs will be covered up. I was told long ago that you can't sue the government. I guess they are right. I have never been able to find a lawyer that would be willing to take on my case, and now too much time has past. I filed a claim with the Veterans Administration (VA) over 30 years ago. PTSD was not known then and my claim was denied. I refilled my claim over 6 years ago and the VA is still dragging my claim out despite all the supporting evidence, tests, pictures and doctor reports that prove my claim true. I know that they want me to just go away or die. I guess this would open up a can of worms the government chooses to bury. I was even told by a VA doctor recently that I should be a little more paranoid. It would be easier to get rid of me and my family than to fix this mess. I feel like a bee (me) trying to sting a dragon (the government) in an attempt to get the dragon's attention. I believe in time the dragon will have to address the bee and take some form of preventative measure to avoid getting stung again from any other bees (others out there with similar experiences). Speaking plainly; the military still has not righted the wrong they did to me. Our children, our sons and daughters who we entrust to our own military, are still being abused by our own military in the same way they were shown abusing the Iraqi prisoners. The military should not be allowed carte blanche to commit a crime and not be held accountable. America is supposed to be the leader of the free world. How can we as a society allow this kind of behavior in our military?

Speaking from first hand experience, rape is a crime that devastates the victim. It also affects close family members and friends of the victim. The psychological and emotional damage is overwhelming and permanent. I clearly understand why most rapes do not get reported. I held on to my private "secret" for over 25 years. I had to block this trauma out of my mind to enable me to go on in life. Only recently, after years of therapy, did I get up the courage to tell my wife, my mother, my daughters and friends. The response was somewhat what I had expected. My wife first told me not to tell my children. My mother told me not to tell my father. My two oldest daughters told me not to tell my other children. My friends told me not to spread it around. It's funny, but they all told me basically to continue to hide this thing without even thinking about the advice they gave me. The strange thing is, the reason they told me not to tell anyone, was that not only were they having a problem handling this, but they assumed none of the people they mentioned would be able to handle it either. How then can society expect a victim to handle it? I had to stop hiding this private secret and share what happened to me. This has to be brought into the light for everyone's good. If everyone keeps quiet evil will continue to spread unchecked.

The Bank Robbery

Chapter 15

When I finally got past my active duty in the service, Ag was home waiting. I was released in January and we married February 1972. I wasn't the same person she knew when I entered the service. I was damaged and she saw it; she knew it. I was an angry, mean and unhappy man now. I didn't like people anymore. I withdrew from my old friends and family. I wasn't looking for new friends. Ag always knew something was wrong with me, but I wouldn't tell her what it was, even with her constant prying. I just wanted to get on with my life with the only person I trusted, my Aggy. I eventually got a job as a bank teller. Ag was working for the phone company. Things seemed to be okay for a little while.

My job working as a teller took place in this small area enclosed with bullet proof glass that went from a counter top up to about two feet below the ceiling. I felt like an animal on exhibit, like an animal in a zoo. One day I was working as the head teller. The head teller had to be sure there was enough cash in the bank to handle the day's payouts. We paid the payroll for several large factories in the area. Thursday and Friday were very busy payroll days. One Thursday I had ordered a few million dollars that would be placed in the vault and then distributed to the other tellers in covering the payrolls. Brinks made the delivery and the day progressed. I had to reopen the vault to restock the tellers. I had the door of the vault closed but it was not locked. There was almost two million dollars in the vault at the time. Then in an instant, like something you would see in a movie, in came these two bank robbers. One of the robbers was flashing a gun. Both robbers were dressed in one piece black and white striped overalls. They were both wearing black ski masks and gloves. The guy with the gun fired a shot at the ceiling while shouting for everyone to get down, this was a hold up. The "this is a hold up," is a mild way of telling you what he said minus all the foul words.

Everyone did as he commanded, everyone but me. I don't know what it is with me. When you grow up living on the streets in a high crime area, hearing gun shots, or hearing about people being shot becomes common place. You just get used to it. After all that I went through in my life I wasn't going to put up with anyone trying to intimidate me. I didn't care how big the gun was, they better shoot to kill, because if they didn't I was still coming for them.

It all happened fast; in fact, it all took place in under two minutes. It seemed like what was happening was a dream. The bank robber without the gun jumped up on the counter and hurled himself over the glass. Then as this was all happening, my PTSD triggered and I felt like I was trapped, just like I was on the ice. I instantly started zoning out and I was back on the ice in my mind. I didn't hear a word either of the bank robbers was saying. Finally the guy with the gun did a totally stupid thing and fired a shot at me and it hit the bulletproof glass. The gun shot shocked me back into reality. Thank God the bullet only ricocheted once and went into the ceiling. It snapped me out of my zoning.

The robber in front of me did not have a gun, and for a moment I thought one left hook or a solid neck blow would easily take this robber out. As I started to advance, the robber holding the gun fired another shot at the ceiling. I immediately turned my attention away from the robber who was standing in front of me to look at the robber holding the gun. He was screaming all kinds of nasty words at me and at the same time he grabbed the secretary by her hair. He was threatening to shoot her if I went near the other robber and did not get down. The secretary was screaming and sobbing hysterically. She was begging me to do what the robbers asked. So I did and the robber that was in the back with me took a chair and bounced it off my back after I got down.

I did not realize it at the time, but my actions had delayed the robbers. They could only get the cash in the tellers' drawers. They did not have enough time to focus on the vault. Someone had hit an alarm button which automatically started the surveillance cameras to shoot in video mode. In each of the tellers' drawers there was also what looked like a regular pack of $10 or $20 bills. It was an exploding dye pack. It was activated in the same way a hand grenade was activated. When the pack was pulled out of the drawer, the pin that kept it from going off, which was attached to the drawer, was pulled out of the pack. Within a short period of time the pack would explode, covering everything in a huge fog of red dye. The robbers had unsuspectingly taken these pacts and put them in the bag with the stolen money.

They had a car waiting and had not even gotten a half mile away when the packs went off. The fog completely filled the car and they couldn't see. They crashed into a fire hydrant. The police were right behind them following the red dye fog trail. The secret service was also called in. We were there all day and well into the night. The guy that did the shooting had the same name as me but his first and middle name were reversed. The guy driving the get away car was Robert Myers, while one of the teller's names was Robbie Myers. Robbie and I kept telling the G-men that we didn't know any of the robbers, nor were we related to them. We ended up going into court as witnesses.

PTSD and Twins

Chapter 16

My PTSD was now becoming a problem. Ever since my assault in the military I will have nightmares. The nightmares usually have white wolves, zombies or a raging mob in them. I am always alone, always vulnerable or naked, always trapped with no way of escape, and I always wake up just as I am being pounced on. When I wake, my heart is pounding and I am covered in sweat. During the day certain things will trigger me and I will zone back to the ice. I have panic and anxiety attacks in crowds. I withdraw from people. I have an inner rage that I do my best to suppress. It never goes away as there was permanent brain damage done. I didn't know it at the time, but I had PTSD or Post Traumatic Stress Disorder. PTSD stays with you. You can't just shake it off or get rid of it, even after years of counseling and medications. I wish I could get rid of it. It's 34 years later and I'm just starting to understand it. I eventually came down with over 100 bleeding ulcers and colitis within the two years after my military duty. I was in and out of the hospital for a while. I had to leave my job at the bank and just work on getting better. The doctors knew it was some kind of nervous anxiety disorder, but nobody knew about PTSD back then.

It was now 1974, just two years after my military release. As the outward manifestation of PTSD were coming to surface, Ag added to my concerns by telling me we were pregnant! The news made me happy and worried at the same time. Shortly after we received the news about the baby, we were told by her doctor that it would be more than one baby and possibly more than two babies. I had just left my job. We had just bought a new house, a new car and now more than one baby in the oven! I had no job and it wasn't long before Ag had to leave hers.

The funny part was the doctor telling me that worrying or stress would only make my (PTSD) anxiety disorder worse. My doctor tried putting me on valiums and librium. I didn't know which end was up. This was not working for me as I could not function. I would not have the ability to work if I was medicated like this. My doctor then told me to try transcendental meditation. I sat in a chair in a comfortable position and relaxed while focusing on an object or word in my mind. I entertained any outside noise and then went back to focusing on the word or object. Eventually I would nod off in a 15 minute power nap. I was to do this twice a day. It was okay at first, but it turned out to be tough to do when we eventually had little ones running around the house. I eventually drifted away from it.

I tried everything to get work. We were losing every material thing we had, but thank God we didn't lose our love for each other. It was no picnic. There were what I will call "heated conversations" and wrongful accusations between Ag and me. It wasn't easy; we sold most everything we had. But through it all we both hung in there. I went back to college at Bridgewater State under the GI bill. The state of Massachusetts paid my tuition so I was bringing in some money. I finally lucked out and got a part-time job with the post office. Ag and I were still far behind in our bills with no real relief in near sight, just trying to survive. Ag was getting bigger. By her size we wondered if there four babies in the oven.

I remember one Sunday I needed to mow the lawn. The lawnmower was out of gas. Back then gas stations were closed on Sundays. So I had an idea. I got a section of hose and stuck it in the gas tank of my car. I figured I would suck on the hose in an attempt to start siphoning some gas. Before I could get the hose out of my mouth I ended up with more than a mouthful of gas. I can not begin to tell you what swallowing gas is like. Saying it is one of the most horrible things you can do is a mild understatement. Please take my advice: do not ever do this! It was a while before I was functional. I did not want to do that again so I came up with another bright idea.

We had this vacuum cleaner that was shaped sort of like an upside down bowl. Someone had given it to Ag and me as a wedding gift. We had never used it. I thought that I could use the vacuum cleaner to start the suction. I would get a longer hose which would give me enough time to shut the vacuum cleaner off before the gasoline reach the vacuum motor. I needed Ag's help though. I told her, "Honey just turn the vacuum on and off real quick. Once we start the suction the gas will flow on its own." I figured if she did it quick nothing would ever explode. I'll never proclaim that Ag or I are the sharpest knives in the drawer. Well, like I said she was pretty big now, being just about seven months pregnant. She was so big she always had to sit down and she could not bend very well. So she sat on top of the vacuum cleaner. Then I told Ag to let it rip! Ag hit the switch, on came the vacuum, then "BOOM!" Ag went pretty high in the air, but the vacuum cleaner left the atmosphere! Okay, so I never knew it was the fumes that exploded. I know now that we could have been hurt. But you had to be there! I was laughing so hard and Ag was struggling to get up off the ground, all the while she was screaming, "Markkkkkk . . . I'm going to kill you! You idiot!" Did you ever laugh so hard you couldn't defend yourself? She chased me around and around the car. I just thank God that she and the babies were fine!

A few months later and Ag gave birth to our twin girls. They were two weeks over due and were both born breech. I know there is medical terminology for this, but basically the birth canal where the baby has to come out of my wife was blocked. So Ag had to deliver the babies by C section. The girls weighed in at a whopping 7 lbs 1 oz. and 7 lbs 8 oz. That's a lot of baby to carry around! Life has some really low times and then this! I can't even begin to express the joy and everything else that went through my mind when the nurse came in and put these two little baby girls in each of my arms. These were my babies and now I was Daddy. "Now what do I do?" I thought. I checked them out thoroughly, making sure they weren't damaged, had all their fingers toes and everything else they were supposed to have. They were perfect. They were born December 24th, 1974. It was the best Christmas present I was ever given and for a brief moment I pondered, maybe there really is a God.

Our Twins

Chapter 17

One of my twins is like a wild stallion. She would always be the one that would kick so hard I thought she would break through my wife's stomach. We named her Danielle Marie. She has always been tough like her old man, but she has her mother's heart. There's a lot of my Italian stubbornness and temperament in this kid. She wouldn't and still won't take any crap from anyone. Once, she was on the all-stars in softball and didn't like the umpire's call. The next thing I remember was both teams trying to pull her off the umpire. Then there was a time when she had a problem with a teacher in high school. She didn't care for him and I don't know what he said to tick her off. I just know she was suspended for jumping right up on his desk and going after him.

    Danielle and I bumped heads a lot. If she got real mad at me she used to lock herself in the second floor bathroom and climb out the window and then drop down two stories off the lower roofs and take off. She would even manage to get out that way when she was supposedly grounded in her room. She would also use that route to climb up and sneak back into the house if I locked the doors. That was an amazing feat in itself. She would sneak in after curfew rather than ringing the doorbell so I wouldn't know what time she got in. No girl would mess with her; neither would most guys. But she did have a child hood sweetheart and ended up marrying him. His name is Joe. I told Joe after he married Danielle there was "no take-sees back." Joe is a great guy with a good nature and a good heart. Joe is a loving husband to my daughter and a great son-in-law. Joe and Danielle have also given me my first grandson, Jacob. He is more joy to me than I can express and he is full of life. I may be partial, but I see a lot of me in this kid.

Our other twin daughter we named Deanna Christine, Dee for short. Dee reminds me of a rose. Looking at Dee and Danielle you would never believe they are twins. Dee has a milder temperament and for the most part is easy going. Dee can have her stubborn moments, when I get to see a little of me coming out. I can only recall one head banging moment I had with Dee as she was growing up. For the most part she made sure that she would keep it on the down low when she was up to mischief. Dee is a different combination of Ag and me. She has my family's passion for chocolate and my taste buds for certain foods. Food is as important to Dee as it is to her dad. Dee has a heart like her mom and ended up taking full guardianship of a little boy who goes by the name of Dylan. Dylan's father is incarcerated. Dylan's mother is a relative who is more interested in heroin and prostitution than she is in looking out for her children. Deanna's heart would not allow her to have Dylan placed in the foster care system. So against my wishes, but in keeping with my wife's wishes, Dee took full guardianship of Dylan. My wife and I are also involved in Dylan's life. Dylan tells Ag and I that he loves us "the most" almost daily.

Dee and Danielle had their battles growing up. The twins are definitely a combination of Ag and me. We see both of us in each one of them. As much as they are different they still end up with similar likes. They even both share their own condos in the same two-family house. They are different as night and day in looks, size and temperament. Danielle is like her mom and can't stand heights. She freaks out going over a bridge. Deanna is more like her dad in the fact that she loves the wild rides, the wilder the better. Dee loves roller coasters and Danielle won't even look at them.

I remember in both their efforts to be different one went

out and bought a red Oldsmobile while the other was out buying a red Buick. Both bought the same year car, same color, in similar condition and similar model. Then a year later both went out not telling the other what they were doing and both ended up trading in their cars the same day at different dealerships for new Hyandi Scoupes. Both cars were exactly the same, including the color. The only difference was one had pink pin striping the other had dark blue pin striping. They had also both returned home within an hour of each other. Weird, isn't it.

Life also has its bright moments. I had Ag and the twins. My life had some really down points and some high ones. I was still trying to bounce back from dealing with the ulcers, colitis and my anxiety disorder. I was still in college and was on a waiting list for a full-time job with the post office. I didn't know it at the time, but something was about to happen that would change my life even more, and forever.

The Encounter with God

Chapter 18

I was still living in Bridgewater with my wife and our twin daughters. I was still looking for a solution to our money problems when I came across an ad for a new business. It involved chemically cleaning brick and stone surfaces. I was so hoping that this new business would be the solution to all our problems. I borrowed $5000 from my in-laws to buy a franchise. By now, the bill collectors were even calling us in the middle of the night. I knew if this new business didn't work we would probably lose our house.

Instead of paying the mortgage I spent the remaining money we had and bought this old van. I needed the van to get the chemicals and a high pressure washer to the job sites. The van was a junk box and I was not a mechanic. It was a mild spring afternoon in 1975 around 2 or 3 o'clock. I had driven this van around to my back yard and had painted the van by hand with a paint brush. It looked better than it did before the paint job. When I finished painting I jumped in and was planning to drive the van to the front of my house. I couldn't get the van to start. I tried everything. This was the last straw! I didn't know what I was going to do. Here I was, 24 years old, with a wife and two young babies. I had no job, we were in debt beyond repayment and the bill collectors wouldn't just go away. I didn't know what to do. I had gone to my in-laws to borrow the money I needed to get this business going and I had no other source I could turn to for help. I was at the bottom or breaking point of my life.

I don't know why, but a thought crossed my mind that maybe I could pray. I couldn't believe a thought like this would ever cross my mind! Me, of all people! Me, pray? To who? To what? To God? I really wasn't even sure there was a God! Then I thought, if there really was a God, why would a superior being even gave a damn? Now I thought I was being ridiculous. If there is a God he must be blind, or he just didn't care! Why, if there is a God and He is this all powerful being doesn't He notice what's going on? Where has He been hiding all my life? Or is it that He just doesn't care, not just about me. Doesn't He see all the suffering in the world! If He is this all compassionate being, how can He face a crippled child? How can He allow babies to have birth defects? How does He allow evil to go unpunished? Maybe He just isn't that powerful after all!

The more I thought about it the angrier I became. At the time I was wrestling with this in my mind I also was noticing my neighbor mowing his lawn and the children of another neighbor playing on their swing set. My thoughts were racing thinking of how much was wrong with this world. How the corrupt seemed to prosper while the good seemed to get crushed. How could there ever be a God? I was becoming furious! If there was a God, He was totally insensitive and removed! Then I did something I would not recommend anyone do. From the bottom of my soul, with every ounce of emotion I could muster, I challenged God! I guess I did this just to really see if anything would happen. I meant business though! I screamed to him, "If you are there, if you exist, I say that you are a coward!" I spit on the ground and stated that I had more respect for the spit than for any blind, self-proclaimed God! I was furious! I screamed out that even I would do a better job than He ever could! I wouldn't allow all the suffering and injustice to continue as was so prevalently seen in the world he supposedly created. "I challenge you God right here, right now, you coward, if you exist, you show me! You prove to me that you exist, or are you afraid of me!" Then everything became very quiet. I looked at my neighbor mowing the lawn, but now I could not hear the mower or hear the children playing on the swing set anymore. I could see, but I could no longer hear.

My back yard was mainly comprised of dense woods. As I faced the woods, I looked in amazement. Though it was quiet, the trees started parting. Not like they were being blown by a gust of wind, but more like something big was coming and pushing them aside like they were twigs! At first I tried to blame it on the wind, but the trees were not bending in the same direction. I could clearly see rows of trees being parted to the left and right at the same time. These were big trees. Whatever it was that was doing this was also heading towards me and I started getting nervous. Then the most amazing thing happened. I can only describe it as a presence that came right up to me from between the trees. This invisible being—yes, I said being—surrounded me and held me frozen just slightly off the ground! There was no mistaking his awesome power as he held me tightly. It was like a powerful energy field that held me as its captive. I could turn my head but my body wasn't able to move! I looked at my neighbor and the children on the swings. I could still see them clearly, but I still could not hear anything! Though I could clearly see all around me, I could not see who held me captive. I felt the presence facing me. There was no question what was happening to me was real. This was no illusion. I was not asleep or in any hypnotic trance. I was not on any medication either, prescribed or otherwise, and I don't drink.

Now I was a lot more than nervous, I was scared! Really scared! I felt like I was an insignificant nothing under the pressure of this being's power. I intensely felt the power and knew He, yes He, could easily crush me in a blink of an eye. His power was immense, so indescribable. The presence was unmistakable! It was similar to an experience where you are in a completely dark room and someone is standing right in front of you. You feel their presence; you know they're there even though you can't see them. There was no mistaking what this being wanted. He made sure that he had my full attention. I was in total awe and wondering in my mind what or who this being was. Then in answer to the question in my mind, I heard a quiet calm voice speaking directly to me. He wasn't angry, though I felt he had every right to be after what I had said. He said, *"I will show you, I am."* He could have crushed me like an ant; instead he took pity on me.

Then I was let go. I fell to the ground and He was gone! I immediately heard my neighbor's lawnmower and the children playing. I was left in total shock and awe! This was no PTSD zoning! This was not a hallucination! This was frightening, exciting and beyond bizarre all in one experience! I was trembling and my mind was racing! What had just happened? I knew what I had just experienced was God! God communicated with me! Why was I allowed this? Why couldn't someone have been with me to witness this event? Regardless, it happened! I wasn't given any new miraculous words, no new golden tablets or tablets of stone, no new hidden secrets and no big poof and now I'm an angel or some holy being. It was just a miraculous experience and the words "I will show you, I am" I will never forget.

But something else happened, although I did not know it at the time. This being "is God" and He planted a seed in me that in time would take root, grow and change me. As I stated, I did not instantly become some perfect being, nor did all of my problems just disappear. But now something was definitely different and I could not get what I experienced or Him off my mind. Now I knew God really did exist. Now I wondered who or what "was I?" His creation? His creature? I didn't know that at the time God knew me. He knew everything about me. He knew every thought and experience I had ever had. He also knew then everything that I would experience in the future. Hind sight is very clear. I know in the present what I did not know in the past. God calls himself "I am."

What I was going to learn from this point on was that God

was going to show me in a way that He knew I would understand. He would show me not only who he was, but who I am. I had a long way to go and lot to learn. But for now I had a burning desire, a longing and a passion to know more! I knew what had just happened to me, definitely happened! I kept asking myself, over and over, 'Why me! Why does the crazy stuff always have to happen to me!" I ran into the house to tell Ag. Of course she thought I had lost my mind and didn't believe me. She was ready to have me committed. From this moment on my life changed! I had to satisfy this new hunger to know more. I had to find out anything and everything I could about God. The God I had experienced, the real God. The God I thought was distant and I probably wouldn't meet until I died, if He did exist. What I was to be shown was more than I knew was possible.

My New Business

Chapter 19

When I was young, I thought I was a good enough person, but I lived a self-centered life. I was more concerned about "what was in it for me" than I was about anyone else around me. Although I had learned there was a God, I still did not know him. I did not yet know who he was or that I was to enter into a personal relationship with him at the time. I did not know that the seed he had planted within me was going to take root and grow. My real world with all of my problems was still there.

I always kept my back yard experience and His words to me in my mind. I would think about God, but I was still living in the real world and I had to concentrate on getting my family out of the mess we were in. I never thought back then to ask God to help me. I knew now there was a God, but I still had not gotten to the point of knowing him. I was still having a problem with the PTSD and decided to seek out professional help in addressing my problem. The doctors in 1975 still did not know about PTSD and treated it as though it was chronic depression coupled with chronic anxiety. They prescribed various antidepressant medicines, but nothing really worked. It didn't just go away. I wished there was a magic bullet, but to date it had not been found. I needed to be alert and fully functional if I was to climb staging and clean the brick faces of buildings. I could not be on medication that was not going to keep me clear headed.

The business I started had more problems than profit. The first job I had was to remove the excess mortar and film left behind when you repoint brick joints. The old fashioned way was to apply diluted muriatic acid with a brush. This had to be done several times to get the brick clean. My way was to apply a biodegradable chemical under low pressure, then wash it off with water under high pressure. My way was at least four times faster than the old way. My first job was a large school and I was to meet the general contractor on Saturday morning. He wanted to see if I could do the job. I had to get rid of the van and managed to scrape up enough money to buy a beat up, but functional pick up truck. I asked two of my brothers to come and help me. I cleaned a small section of the building that was freshly pointed. The contractor was impressed, and asked if I could stay the rest of the day and also work Sunday. We agreed on a price. Money was money and I definitely needed it.

By Saturday evening we had cleaned almost one quarter of the school. We came back on Sunday and by evening we had half the job done. I was happy with the progress and figured this business might be okay after all. Then I showed up on Monday with my two brothers. This time there was a large group of construction gorillas there to meet us. They were not happy. About a dozen of these guys had surrounded the truck and of course they had a guy with a tie and a clipboard there with them. The guy with the tie was the union representative. He asked me if I was the one who cleaned the building. I, of course, being proud of the work I did, said yes. It was then explained to me that this was a union job and I was not in their union. While the rep was explaining this to me, the gorillas were in the process of throwing all of my equipment out of the truck. They were not being very gentle. My brothers got out of the truck before the gorillas tipped it over.

I was trying to negotiate with the guy in the tie to get out of this deal before my equipment and the truck were not the only things that got damaged. I knew very well who ran the unions and I was not about to break any family rules. I called the general contractor and told him the problem. I could not finish the job as I was not allowed to. I wanted to be paid for the work that I did and end this mess. He stated he didn't care about the union; that was my problem. If I didn't finish the job he wasn't going to pay me. Seeing that he was unreasonable I decided to tell him that I just needed time to work it out with the union rep and would call him back.

    I told the rep that I did not want to cross any lines and wanted to get off the job. I asked if there was some way I could appease the union. The rep told me that I had to put three of his guys on the payroll. They also didn't have to work. I just had to pay them the union wage. I agreed if they could tip my truck back over and help me get my equipment straightened out. I then called the general contractor back and told the slime ball that I worked everything out with the union. I just needed some up front money to buy more chemicals to finish the job. He agreed to the amount I asked for. I left my brothers at the job and went to pick up the check. I told my brothers not to use any more chemicals and not to clean anything else. I told them to just keep spraying water on the bricks until I got back.

    I met the general contractor and picked up a sizable check. It was more than adequate to cover my losses and I ran to the bank. I cashed the check and went back to the job site. I called my brothers off the scaffolding and told them to pack up the truck. The rep came over and I put a couple of 100's in his hand and said "Arrivederci." When the general contractor found out I was gone he was furious. He called me and I explained in no misunderstood terms that he was a slime ball and he could now take up any problems with the union.

    There were a few small jobs after that. I never did anything like this before and mostly ended up losing more than I ever made. Then I got a call from a contractor out of Providence, RI. He wanted me to clean a stone statue of a Polish general that stood in the middle of Chelsea Square. I figured I could make some quick money and we came to terms. I had my cousin working with me that day. A town alderman showed up at the job site. He told me I wasn't doing any work until I talked to him back at his office. I told my cousin to set up the equipment, but to not do anything else until I returned. When I met with the alderman I found out he was looking for a pay out. I refused and said he could clean the statue himself. I left his office and went back to meet up with my cousin. My cousin thought he was doing me a favor and started to spray the statue with the chemical. He didn't know how concentrated the chemical was and that it had to be diluted to 50 parts water. I arrived just in time to see General Pulaski's head melting of its shoulders. We got out of there fast.

My Cousin Brian

Chapter 20

One of the things the chemicals I was using in this business were supposed to do was to strip paint. It did not do this well and most surfaces had to be sand blasted. I rented a compressor and tried out sand blasting paint off of small things. It took practice working with the various sand grades to learn what a sand blaster can do.

It was a warm day in July. I landed a fairly good size job stripping the exterior paint off a historic house in Milton. I had my cousin Brian working with me. He didn't mind the heat or the suit you had to wear to protect yourself from the ricocheting sand. My cousin was up on the scaffolding sand blasting the house and I was on the sidewalk working the compressor. You can't get close to the shooting sand as it can strip off your skin in a fraction of a second. Things were going okay, then, as though we were watching a commercial, these three gorgeous girls came walking down the street. They all had on bikini tops and hot pants. Nature had been very generous to them. My cousin, who is also very Italian, noticed them just as quickly as I did. The compressor was still running at full speed and my cousin still had the sand blasting gun open at full blast. He was watching the girls and not what he was doing. He was turning this way and that trying to get a long look at the girls. He didn't realize he was destroying the house. He was shattering windows and destroying the furniture inside the house. He was swinging the sand blasting gun all over the place, including at me standing next to the compressor. He was blocking me from getting to the compressor to shut it down. I was screaming at him but he couldn't hear me. I then tried to hit him with rocks to get his attention. I finally hit him and he shut down the gun.

He was mad at me because I had hit him with a rock. I finally got him to wake up and see what he did. Thank God, the owners were away. The house was a wreck. It looked like the work of the "Three Stooges." It was late and we had to do something about the mess. My cousin said he was tired and was going home. I told him he better meet me here tomorrow to fix all of this. He said, "Tomorrow's Sunday. I want double time or I'm not coming." I wanted to strangle him, but he took off on his motorcycle before I had the chance. This one put me out of business. I guess I wasn't destined to be on this road. I still had not figured out that God has his hand in everything.

I couldn't stay mad at my cousin Brian. He is a lot like me. My uncle Frank, Brian's father, is a full blown Italian with a vicious temper. Brian has a hearing disorder. He, like me, was rejected by his family. He was always getting into mischief and his father would always beat him. I remember witnessing this one time in particular along with my other cousins. We were all over at my grandmother's house. I don't remember what Brian did to set his father off. I do remember that my uncle had the three foot metal vacuum cleaner extension pipe in his hand. Brian was pinned down on the floor as my uncle repeatedly beat him with that pipe. We were all horrified, screaming and crying for my uncle to please stop. When he did stop Brian just looked up at him and said, "Is that the best you got old man!" Brian definitely had moxie. Of course, my uncle then resumed the beating. When he stopped, Brian heckled him again. This went on and on until my other uncles came out and got my uncle to stop. Brian has grown up to be a very caring person. I am grateful to have him as my cousin. He is also a very good architect that has designed many buildings in Boston. He helped me tremendously in designing my house. It's the dream house my wife has always wanted.

My Adriana

Chapter 21

Shortly after my business loss, I started getting more hours in at the post office. Now I was getting in around 30 to 40 hours a week, and some of the financial pressure was slowly being relieved. Then I found out "we" were pregnant again. By the due date the baby was still in the oven and we still had a blocked birth canal. So two weeks after the due date Ag went in for another C section. Fathers were not allowed in the operating room back then, so I waited in Ag's room like I did when the twins were born.

We didn't know if we were having a boy or a girl. The only thing we were sure of was that if we had another girl her name would be Adriana. I remember that I saw this name on the back of a boat and thought it was a pretty name for a girl.

It was January 6, 1977. January 6th is also known as Little Christmas or, "Nollaig Bheag" in the Irish language. It is one of the traditional names commonly known as the Epiphany. It is so called because it was, until the adoption of the Gregorian calendar, the day on which Christmas Day was celebrated. It is the traditional end of the Christmas season and the last day of the Christmas holidays for both primary and secondary schools. It is also known as Women's Christmas (Nollaig na mBan). It is so called because of the tradition of Irish men taking on all the household duties on that day and giving their spouses a day off.

I waited in Ag's room, and continued to wait, and waited some more, but still no baby. It had been hours. The twins had not taken this long. I was beginning to panic and worry. Finally a nurse showed up, but there was no baby with her! "Mr. Lynch I need you to please come with me," she said.

"What do you mean come with you, where's my baby! Is my wife all right? What's wrong?" I asked. She wouldn't tell me anything. She was telling me to please calm down and come with her. We both got into the elevator and she pushed B for basement, not 2 for second floor where they kept the babies. We got off the elevator and started down a corridor. She was still avoiding my questions. I was starting to get angry. We now walked to this area that was full of incubators. I saw little babies in the incubators, babies that were hooked up to tubes. My heart was wrenching and now I was really worried.

We were now in front of the door that led into the area that had the incubators. The nurse told me to wait outside this area. There was a guard and an orderly standing at the door. Now I was starting to freak out in anger. I told the guard to get out of my way and started heading toward the door. The guard tried to stop me. I wasn't in the mood to be stopped. I just grabbed him and threw him down the hallway. I did the same to the orderly as he approached me. I was now screaming, "Where's my wife, where's my baby!" In an instant a doctor ran over to me. He told the guard and orderly that it was okay to let me by. He was telling me if I calmed down he would take me to my baby. He told me my wife was okay, but my baby was in trouble. He then made me put on sterile hospital clothes and brought me over to this incubator. He told me I could watch if I remained calm while the doctors worked on my baby. I had tears in my eyes as I looked into the incubator and saw my baby girl. She was so swollen, blown up like a balloon. Her whole body was a dark black purple, except for a small pink area around her nose and mouth.

My head was swimming and all I could do was focus on what was before me. I felt so helpless. I watched the doctors as the miracle in front of my eyes played out. Slowly the pink area grew larger and larger as the dark purple areas started to change to pink. Now the only dark purple on her body was in her fingers and toes. I watched and cried. Then she started crying and they let me put my hand inside the incubator and touch her. I kept saying to her over and over, "Its okay baby, Daddy's here." She stopped her crying and I cried even more. She had swallowed the am bionic fluid.

About a week later she was all pink and we all left the hospital. I didn't know it when I named her, but Adriana means the water bearer. From the day she was born and every day since, this girl always has a bottle of water in her hand. She doesn't like milk, she only drinks water. Weird, isn't it? I know now it was God who named her.

Adri is also a different combination of Ag and I. Adri is flamboyant and always has a big smile. She is my little miss sunshine and my little princess. She was spoiled more than the twins. She always had to carry around this smelly stuffed rabbit and a blanket. She walked around with one finger in her mouth and one finger up her nose. She always had this red rash around her mouth from sucking on her fingers so much. Thank God she outgrew that. She was into singing and dance recitals. She would wear bright colored clothes with large stripes or dots. You could tell it was her from a mile down the road. Adri always had to have me carry her or she always would end up sitting on my lap wanting my full attention. Even now she steals my sweatshirts from my closet. I bought her her own sweatshirts so she would stop taking mine. She still won't give me mine back. She says she needs mine. She doesn't even wash them first. Yeah, it makes me smile. Actions speak what's really in the heart.

Adri would never need to be told twice when she was being bad. I never had to really yell at Adriana. She would always bring home the "A's" from school. Adri's all grown up now. She's a first grade school teacher and married to another great son-in-law. His name is Sean. Sean also has a big heart. He is like this huge little kid. Sean spoils my daughter in the manner she has become accustomed too. Sean still calls his mom and dad every night just to tell them he loves them. Adri loves little kids and little kids love Adri. Adri and Sean are soon to give birth to my second grandchild. Everyone in the family thinks she is having a boy. I told her that God told me she would be having a girl and her name would be Isabella Grace. Shortly thereafter, Adri and Sean couldn't hold the news back any longer and told us all that the baby is going to be a girl. Adri and Sean told me that they have also chosen to call her Isabella Grace. She is my Bella Mia Grace, my beauty and grace from God.

Darwin's Joke

Chapter 22

It was about this time in my life when my thoughts kept going back to the experience I had in meeting God. Over the next few years I started a serious quest seeking God out. I had to find out for myself who he really was. I eventually found him and later learned this can only be done through Jesus Christ, God the son. I originally began my quest in finding the true God by checking out everything I could at the library. I remembered learning about Roman and Greek gods in school. The God I sought was not to be found there. It was like praying to rocks or wooden idols seeking answers. Like we say in Italian, "faa–geta–bout–it," a big waste of time. For those who haven't figured it out yet, the Roman and Greek gods (little "g"), rocks and wooden idols won't respond. I knew that I would not find the God I sought here.

I also knew that Darwin's theory was a joke; it was so easy to disprove. All life and things were created from the factual existence of DNA. I know this for certain as a State of Massachusetts Department of Education certified Mathematics and Earth Science teacher. The greatest scientists throughout our time know that Darwin's theory is a joke. Darwin's theory is not even real science. For those who don't know why it's called a theory, it's because there are "no facts" to back it up. It's basically a guess. It is just as good of a guess as in believing that we all came from aliens from outer space. As for the creation, there is quite a bit of factual evidence proving creation to be a fact opposed to it being a theory. I am amazed at all the people out there that still choose to believe in Darwin.

Darwin himself stated that there "is not" now, nor has there ever been any physical evidence of any cross bred mutated species. In simple terms, there is no evidence that any monkey ever turned into a human, and a duck will never become a horse, no matter how long a time period or how much cross breeding between species is tried. Darwin himself was saying his theory was junk. I know common sense is not very common, but this theory is so ridiculous I am amazed that this trash is still being taught in most public schools. The real facts are that people just don't want to believe there is, or they don't want to be controlled by, God. Why, if they believed the truth and God did exist, this would interfere with what they know is wrong. Sexual freedom would be out the window. Therefore, they would rather hang on to their ignorance. What I was to learn and know for certain that these people fail to realize is whether they like it or not God still controls everything, including them.

Let's get back to good old Darwin. Java man and all the other deformed humanoids that were found "in the singular" were just that: deformed humanoids. Has the reader ever heard of the elephant disease, or seen a mongoloid person, a midget, or someone with a deformity? These are genetic mutations of humans, not apes. For those that still want to hang on to Darwin I would ask if you ever really thought of the following: If mankind came from apes, where did the apes come from? If you can answer that one, then where did that thing come from and so on? Think about this: Darwin's missing link would have to have been missing "links." Not an ape man, but ape "men," tribes of them. To complicate this a little more there would have to be both male and female of these things. If Darwin was right there would also have to be tadpole ducks, tadpole dogs, tadpole lizards, tadpole trees and so on. Not just one, but a whole big bunch of them, male and female. If you really get to the meat of Darwin's theory and put it in a nutshell,

Darwin stated that given enough time, and all by itself, "spit" or "dust" (basically bacteria, dirt and water) will turn into a duck, or a horse, or a tree, or even you the reader. But then we would still be stuck with the question, "Were did the spit or dust come from?"

In Darwin's time they did not know about DNA. DNA, carbon dating and forensic science prove Darwin was a joke. Darwin would have really had a hard time explaining DNA if he was still around; but then he's probably a pile of "dust" by now. DNA is in everything. This is known, proven scientific fact, not a theory! This fact alone proves Darwin's theory is wrong. If you study DNA you will find it has a binary code. A binary code is what we use today to make computers "think." It requires an intelligent life form, "a creator." Binary code does not create itself!

If Darwin's theory were correct, in this day and age we could easily create the creatures found only in the far out tabloids. The "dog man," a creature that is half dog and half man. The "tree horse," a creature that is half tree and half horse. The combinations would be endless. If Darwin were right all of this would be possible. Science has not been able to cross breed species, because it cannot be done. The truth is the only mating that can successfully occur is the breeding of things of the same kind. Human breeding of any national origin only begets humans. Humans cannot mate with anything but humans. Attempting to do so produces nothing. Humans cannot mate with apes, dogs, sheep, chickens, trees, or anything other than humans. We can cross breed dogs, but we still end up with a dog. It may be a combination of breed, but it's still a dog. The same applies to cats, horses, trees, and on and on. Breeding of "same kinds," works, breeding of "different kinds," cannot be done. I also found out later that the Bible states only the reproduction of the "same kind" or "same species" will work (note: Genesis 1:24 NIV). We also know this as scientific fact today, not as a theory. It can be proven. If its goes against the stubborn grain to believe there is a God, don't waste time on Darwin. It would be better to believe that we all came from aliens; but then how will you explain where the aliens came from?

Then I pondered another thought. First, imagine a person like Darwin getting a doctorate in anthropology. After all that hard work getting the degree, where could someone like Darwin find employment? Darwin had to eat. I would imagine someone with Darwin's credentials would end up as a professor in some university or college if there were enough jobs and they were hiring. These jobs also don't pay very much. I know this by having personal experience in the teaching profession. Or perhaps the individual could be backed by some foundation or museum that would be willing to send them out to find the answers to the origin of man. After a few years, if they didn't come up with something, I can certainly see the foundation or museum losing hope and the thought of funding further research is quickly going out the window. So, if it was me being funded, I would come up with something, anything! Unemployment is untasteful! Being an unsuccessful, unemployed Doctor of Anthropology would not be good. So bring on "Java Man," or even "Peking Duck"! Whatever it takes! Just show me the money! I'd find whatever they would pay me to find! Why, look, here's the missing link. Java man, or Coffee man, whatever they want to call it! It would easily fool those seeking anything but God. Why, we could use pig bones, monkey or ape bones, and mix them with some deformed human bones. A little shaping with stones, soak it all in a little dye for aging, maybe mix the whole lot with some old volcano ash. The intelligence of the "so called" intelligent has always astounded me. How can people be so silly and foolish? People would rather believe in a lie then turn to the truth?

Various Beliefs

Chapter 23

Knowing for certain that God was alive, I needed to find who he really was. I had to research all of the mainline religions to be sure I didn't miss anything and was correct in my facts. I remember my past being raised as a Catholic. I was never really taught about "knowing God." I was only taught about "knowing of God." Even the devil and all his angels "know of God." The Roman Catholic Church taught me about the Trinity. They taught me how Jesus was brutally crucified on the cross. But they never explained it all or what it all was about. I remember a lot of what I was shown and taught as a Roman Catholic. I also remember why I left this organization. I never found a personal God in this organization. I have much more to say about the Roman Catholic Church, but first I need to address some of the well known cults.

    I studied other various popular religious organizations. I wanted to understand what they believed to be the truth in searching for God. I read a lot, listened a lot and asked a lot of questions. If you really want to know the truth, you can find it if you truly seek it out. I researched the Unitarians, the Mormons, Jehovah Witness, Buddhism and the Hindu beliefs. They all claimed to be right. So, I figured I needed to check them all out before I ruled them out and to be sure I was on the right track. I needed to pay closer attention, to listen exactly to what they all had to say and see if I could find the real God, the

God who I experienced in my back yard. I knew that although He was invisible, He certainly was very much alive. I felt if I could find Him again, and it was definitely a "Him" and not a "her," I could get answers to a lot of my questions.

This may not be politically correct, but for the sake of the elect I must comment on what I did learn. I remember reading a bulletin board posted outside a Unitarian Church. It said that God is alive and well and that the pastor of this church knew this because she had just talked to "her" this morning. The God that I met in my back yard was certainly not feminine. I found that the Unitarian Church has no real rules. Basically, an individual can believe anything they want. If it feels good then it's okay. How can you expect to truly find God when you limit God to your own personal agenda? The true God I met cannot be contained.

Christian Scientists deny sin, evil, sickness and death. They do not believe in the need for salvation as they believe there is nothing to be saved from. The Unitarians deny the deity of Christ. The Mormons and Jehovah Witnesses are basically twisted off shoots of Christianity. They keep changing their organization's rules and regulations because they are constantly being proven how far off target they are. I read the book of Mormon and the Watchtower. I talked to various members and leaders. All of these organizations were formed long after the well accepted Christian Bible was published.

The Mormons and Jehovah Witnesses were both founded by individuals. The individuals that started these organizations both claim to have had "a new and personal revelation from God" and published an additional "testament." This of course is strictly forbidden if you read the last chapter of the original wildly accepted Bible (note: Revelations 22:18, 19 NIV). The individuals could not or did not perform anything miraculous that you would expect to find with God. Joseph Smith was the founder of the Mormon religion back in 1823. This was long after the Holy Bible was written. Smith states in the introduction of the Book of Mormon that it is "a volume of the Holy Scripture comparable to that of the Bible." Did you note the word "comparable"? Charles Russell started the Jehovah's Witness back in 1884 much like Smith did. Russell's big claim to fame is the "Watchtower." Both of these organizations took the widely accepted Bible and twisted, deleted or added words to fit their liking, or personal agenda.

The best lie is the one that is closest to the truth. A lie may contain portions of truth, but in the end the lie is revealed as simple twisted truth. Today you would commonly find the twisted truth in our courts spoken by lawyers and judges. You will also find the twisted truth spoken by many politicians. In fact it was the twisted truth that was used by Satan to get Eve to eat the forbidden fruit. The Mormons and Jehovah Witnesses are constantly being proven wrong about taking things out of context and making predictions that always fail to happen. Both the book of Mormon and the Watchtower are filled with contradictions. They are their own worst enemy and cannot be taken seriously if you really want to seek out the one, and only one, true God. They profess to be Christian based organizations, but when you get into "the meat" of the club rules and regulations, both are organizations that professes entrance to heaven can only be obtained through an individual's good works and thus they nullify what Jesus actually did for mankind when he was crucified on the cross and prove their organizations to be false.

I found both Buddhism and Hinduism to be basic fairy tales. Buddha came onto the scene around 600 BC. At that time the people were a little upset with the animal sacrifices by the priests. This was a standard Jewish custom at the time, by the way. Buda came along with a fairy tale that any individual could have made up. I guess it was a case of being in the right place at the right time. Buda never performed any miracles or did anything proving him to be God or worthy of any worship. But people still bought what Buda was selling just like they buy Darwin. They needed an alternative; they were not going to allow themselves to be controlled by any God that interfered with the way they wanted to live. But the reality is that Buda's dust can be found in the grave of Buda.

In Hinduism you will find the Rig Veda. This is comprised of mainly hymns to the "gods." They are still back there with the Romans and the Greeks living in a flat world. What I did find in all of the above noted religions were major human flaws. If there are easily proven flaws within an organization's foundation, then sooner or later the organization will fall apart. If you are serious about seeking God you won't find the true God in any of these noted organizations. Again, please note the warning about all this as stated in the Bible in the book of Revelations 22:18 and 19 (NIV).

Jewish or Muslim

Chapter 24

In continuing my quest for understanding in my search for "The true God," I also checked out the Jewish beliefs of the Israeli people and the Muslim beliefs of the Arab people. The Jewish people have the Hebrew Bible and the Muslims have the Quaran or Koran as the foundations of their belief system. So I researched the Hebrew Bible and The Muslim Koran.

The Hebrew Bible contains the Torah as well as most of what is comprised in the Old Testament of the widely accepted Bible. Both the Israelis and the Arab nations come from the same seed, the seed of Abraham. Both nations of people started long ago with a promise made by God to Abram. God promised Abram that he would have a son. God promised Abram that he was to be the father of a great nation. Through Abram's family line would eventually come the Messiah. Abram was around 100 years old at the time and his wife Sarah was around 90 years old. I don't know what Abram was thinking, perhaps he thought Sarah was a little too old to have a baby, or that there was no way she could get pregnant. Anyway, Abram messed things up as he figured he would help God out and hurry things up a bit and he impregnated Sarah's maidservant. Sarah's maidservant Hagar produced a son, and he was named Ishmael.

Explained in a little more detail, God chose Abram to be the father of all of "God's children." God changed Abram's name from Abram to Abraham. Abraham knew God. Abraham didn't just know of God. Throughout Abraham's life Abraham proved his "trust and faith" in God. Abraham's trust and faith in God pleased God and God accepted Abraham. Without trust and faith in God you cannot please God.

This trusting in God goes back to the beginning of the Bible (note: Genesis 3 NIV) with Adam and Eve proving by their actions that they did not trust God. God told Adam and Eve not to eat the fruit from the tree of knowledge. Then Adam and Eve ate the forbidden fruit from the tree of knowledge. In doing what God strictly told them not to do they both showed that they doubted God. Better put; they showed by their example that they did not trust or did not believe what God said. This is a "lack of faith," which God is most displeased with. Only by having "trusting faith acted out sincerely" can we please God.

Eve was tempted to do what God told her not to do by Lucifer the devil or serpent. The temptation was not where Eve went wrong as temptation is common to us all. It is only when we let the temptations take root in our minds and "we then act" on them does it become sin. Eve sinned, or showed that she did not trust or believe God, when she trusted in what Lucifer, the devil or Satan, had tempted her with. She acted on it by eating the forbidden fruit. Adam sinned when he trusted his wife instead of trusting god and acted on it when he then ate the forbidden fruit. Adam and Eve had it made in paradise. They had a relationship with God and God was with them in the garden of paradise. When Adam and Eve sinned they were expelled from paradise. Today we can only get to be with God "by grace through faith, and that not of ourselves" Ephesians 2: 8–9. Simply put, we get "into paradise" by our belief, trust and faith in God. We also cannot save ourselves.

Let me get back to Abraham. God told Abraham he would give him a son even though Abraham was around 100 years old. Abraham, persuaded by his wife Sarah I might add, figured he would help God out in fulfilling God's promise of granting him a son. But as I stated several times before, God means what he says and says what he means. God did not need or ask for Abraham's help. Abraham then slept with Sarah's maidservant Hagar, supposedly thinking he was doing the right thing. Imagine a 100 year old man taking on this tough assignment in helping out God. Where he ever thought it was right is beyond me.

Hagar became pregnant and had a baby boy named Ishmael. God never promised Abraham that Ishmael was the baby God was talking about, or the legitimate baby Abraham should have had with Sarah his wife. The baby God promised was to be first born of the nation we now know as Israel. The baby born of Abraham and Sarah would be named Isaac. Even though Ishmael was the first son of Abraham's seed he was also illegitimate. Isaac was the first born legitimate son of Abraham and Sarah. God clearly states throughout the Old Testament that the Messiah, the Savior of mankind would be a descendent of Isaac, not Ishmael. Hagar and Ishmael were sent away by Abraham into the desert where they should have died. What a great thing for Abraham to do? God, being merciful, did not allow them to die in the desert. God, being more merciful than Abraham, heard Hagar's cries and spared her and her son. God also promised to make Ishmael the first born of another nation of peoples. Ishmael turned out to be the first born and founder of the Arab tribes, the Arab nation, the foundation of Islam, ancestor to Mohammad and the Muslim religion. This is also where the Arab and Israeli feud began that continues to this day. Mohammad entered the picture in 610 A.D. (after the death of Christ) not B.M. (before Mohammad).

Mohammad stated that for 22 years of his existence he was given revelations from God. The Koran is comprised of these revelations. The Koran does not read like a story. It is mainly a bunch of sentences that do not lead anyone anywhere. They appear as though they are spoken from an individual under some hypnotic trance or possession. They are sentences or fragmented sentences bent mostly toward violence. The God I met in my back yard could have crushed me like a bug. But he didn't. Instead He stated to Me, "*I will show you, I Am.*"

I admit I was a total idiot in challenging a God I was not sure even existed. It happened at the lowest point in my life when I felt that straw that broke the camel's back and I was screaming out in desperation. Instead of crushing me, the God I met had mercy and compassion on me. He knew I had no clue and did not understand anything. I know now what he was saying to me. *"I will show you, I Am,"* meaning I will teach you so that you understand, for I am God, the only God. The God of Islam is not the merciful or compassionate God I met; in fact, the God of Islam is just the opposite. There is an opposing force to the true God that is led by a powerful being. His given name was Lucifer; you may know him as Satan or the devil. He and his fallen angel followers, known as demons, have the ability to possess humans. Mohammad himself never did anything miraculous and never claimed to be God, and I do suspect he was possessed.

It is factual that both the Arabs and the Jews came from the same seed of Abraham, both believe in a God and both have a very violent history, as do most all the major religions. The sad part is both the Arab Muslim nation and the Israelis for the most part missed the mark when they both noted a coming messiah, but overlooked or did not accept the fact that Jesus is that true messiah. You can find the information concerning the Jewish people in the Old Testament of the Bible or in the Hebrew Bible. As for Islam, I suggest you just read the Koran for yourself to fully comprehend my understanding.

Strongly feeling that Islam was not taking me in the direction I needed to go, I was led to further my study of the God of Abraham, Isaac, Jacob, Moses and David and Daniel; the God of the Jewish people. All of the individuals mentioned were "sinners," yet all of these individuals knew God, trusted, believed and put all of their faith in God. There is a big emphasis throughout the entire Bible about this trusting faith in God. They all proved they had this trusting faith throughout their lives. These individuals as well as others played a major role in the history of the Israeli nation. The more that I read the more that I learned and the more I was convinced that this is where I would find the one and only real God. My passion to know and understand was being fed and leading me to the true God. Through the Jewish religion I was lead to the True God. This then lead me to not just God the Father, but also to God the Holy Spirit and God the Son. God the Son is Jesus, the Messiah, the true Savior of all those who choose to believe in him and trust him.

I began a deep concentration of studying the entire Bible. The Bible is one book that contains 66 books in total and is comprised of the Old and New Testaments. The Old Testament is comprised of 39 books of the Jewish writings or the writings of the Hebrew Bible. In the Old Testament we find the beginning of the human race, interactions of God with the Jewish nation, parts of the history of the Jewish nation, and most importantly many areas where the Old Testament points to the Messiah, the Savior, the Lord Jesus Christ, God the Son. The Bible also contains 27 books of the New Testament. Here we find the Ministry of Jesus. You will find miracles that only God could do. Only some of all the miracles that were done by Jesus are recorded. Jesus performed these miracles which, were witnessed by thousands upon thousands of people. The miracles proved that Jesus was the Son of God. In the New Testament we also find the writings of the works of his followers, his apostles and disciples. Finally in the last book within the Bible we find the book of Revelation. The book of the Revelation is the book where you will find the things to come and the end of this world.

In Christianity, I could not find the same flaws that I found in any of the human originated religions. In fact I could not find any flaws. I only found that the Bible to be the true inspired word of God. Every word in the Bible is true and right on the money. The New Testament is where I learned not only about the miracles Jesus performed, but what he taught his followers concerning who God is, who we are and what God expects from us in a relationship intended to last an eternity.

Roman Catholic Traditions

Chapter 25

As I learned the truth, I reflected back on what I thought I knew. As I stated earlier I was raised as a Roman Catholic. I was married in an Albanian Orthodox Catholic Church, simply to please my new wife. I know the Orthodox Church as well as I know the Roman Catholic Church. Now I am known as a Protestant Christian. As I stated earlier, as a Roman Catholic I was never deeply taught the things that I now was finding out as I read the Bible. Again, I was told about Jesus, God the Trinity, Mary the mother of Jesus, but not taught about God to the depth I was now discovering. Yes! There really is a God. He's not dead, deaf, or blind by any means. The true God is one God made of three persons, if you can grab all that: the Father, Son and Holy Spirit. I know I can't totally understand it, but then I am only human and being human means I have a limited brain capacity. It is all true just the same.

I first would like to clearly emphasize in addressing the Roman Catholic church, it is first and foremost a Christian rooted organization. Many members of the one "true church" can be found within the Roman Catholic Church. But the Roman Catholic Church as an organization is not in itself the one church of God that it professes itself to be. When I was raised as a Roman Catholic I was taught to believe certain things. The foundation and beginning of the Roman Catholic Church is based on Christianity as it is presented in the Bible. Over time this organization has changed. The Roman Catholic Organization added a lot of man made, not God made, rules and regulations. It is interesting what the profit Isaiah (Isaiah 29:13–14 NIV) states about matters like this in the Old Testament: "The Lord says, "These people worship me only with their words, they Honor me by what they say. But their hearts are far away from me. Their worship doesn't mean anything to me. They teach nothing but human rules."

My family ancestry was Roman Catholic, so in lazy fashion and in keeping with tradition, so was I. I was told that if I ever swayed from the Roman Catholic Church my soul was doomed to hell. The Roman Catholic Church was the only road to salvation. What a crock of baloney. I believed this was the straight deal at the time. I know now I was naive and gullible. Growing up I was told only priests could read the Bible; it was forbidden for lay people to read it. We lay people would only get confused; we simply needed to trust the priests. This is where I and most people make a big mistake. Isaiah 29:11–12 (NIV) states a prophecy from God: "For you this whole vision is nothing but words sealed in a scroll. And if you give the scroll to someone who can read, and say to him, 'Read this, please,' he will answer, 'I can't; it is sealed.' Or if you give the scroll to someone who cannot read, and say, 'Read this, please,' he will answer, 'I don't know how to read.' Simply put, ignorance is either bliss or chosen.

God's word or the Bible was translated into Latin, the language of the Romans, from the Hebrew and Aramaic by Jerome between 382 and 405 A.D. and was known as the Vulgate. The Vulgate was the standard version of the Bible for Roman Catholics for over one and a half millennia. Since Latin was only studied by priests and scholars, the vast majority of people could not read or understand the Vulgate. Back when the Roman Catholic Church first began, most people could not read or write. The people would gather in a large group, or putting it another way, "a mass of people would gather together."

This is most likely why the worship service performed by the priests is known as a mass today. The priests who could translate Latin, Greek, Aramaic and/or Hebrew would deliver the message. It was supposed to be the teachings that anyone can find in the standard widely accepted Bible of today. This practice of getting a mass of people together became a tradition. Since most of the people could not read or write they trusted that the priests were giving them the straight scoop. The priests being human were and are flawed as much as every other human. Sometimes things were taken out of context, sometimes things were said that are not found in the Bible. Then sometimes the priests would take advantage of the people's trust.

The Vulgate was the main Bible used until the Protestant Reformation in the 14th and 15th centuries when the Bible was finally translated into modern languages, against the great resistance from the leadership of the Roman Catholic Church. The resistance by the Roman Catholic leadership is understandable, as ignorant people are easily manipulated. The Roman Catholic leadership did not want the whole truth to be known, as it would diminish their power over the people. It would also diminish their treasury. I know when I was growing up there were a lot of "thou's and shalt's" in the Bible with an old English translation, and it made for tough reading. But that has all changed and anyone can read the Bible and fairly understand it today with the new translation Bibles. So no one really has an "excuse" for not knowing or at least not checking out the Bible.

I used to believe as do most other lay people that belonging to this religious organization, saying a few repetitive prayers and occasionally attending church was enough to get me into heaven. In my Roman Catholic upbringing I was taught that breaking any of the Ten Commandments or any other rule or regulation of the Roman Catholic Church was a sin. It wasn't until I did the research that I found out that most of the man made rules, regulations and traditions made up by the Roman Catholic Church could not be found in the Bible.

I was originally taught by the Roman Catholic Church to

believe that sin came in two forms: venial and mortal. Committing a mortal sin meant that there was no hope for me and I was going straight to hell when I died. If I was sent to hell it was a place of fire and here I would meet some red guy known as the devil. The devil had horns, a tail, a pitch fork and he was very bad. If I avoided a mortal sin I would be okay. There were times that I didn't know for sure if I had committed a mortal sin and I was doomed. A venial sin could be forgiven if it was confessed to a priest. I would go into this closet like box and knelt on a padded cushion. The priest would be in an adjoining closet like box. Between the two boxes was an area of smoked glass or plastic with holes in it. I would have to tell the priest what sins I had committed through the smoked glass during the period of time that I last went through this ritual. I would be told by the priest to say a standard prayer of contrition and then the priest would award me with some penance to perform. Then the priest, supposedly standing in for God (as if some mere human ever could), would absolve you of your sin.

Most penance was in the form of repeating the standard Roman Catholic prayers, like the Hail Mary, which can't be found in the Bible, or the Our Father, which can be found in the Bible, several times over and over. The priest decided how much and what penance was required. I could whip though those prayers in no time and be out of there. None of it had any real meaning for me. I was also brought up to believe that you never eat meat on Friday as it also was a sin. I did not know it at the time but found out later that this is another man made rule, not God's rule. I had hoped this was a venial sin, as I loved hamburgers and steak any day of the week. I used to confess this one often and since the priest stated I was absoloved I figured it had to be a venial sin. I found out something entirely different written in the Bible. What I found out to be the truth that is found in the Bible is in God's eyes sin is sin, period.

I used to believe knowing of God was enough. I never thought that God would ever be a personal God. God was some distant, unreachable being that you met at the end of your life. The Roman Catholic Church also taught me about this place called purgatory. This was an in-between place where my would be held for a period of time depending on how ba was in this life. I was taught to believe that if I did not measure up with a fair balance of good deeds outweighing my bad deeds, my spirit just floated around in purgatory until the Apostle Peter, who held the keys to heaven, thought I waited around long enough and let me enter heaven or Peter thought I was never going to get into heaven and he would send me off to hell. In purgatory I was expected to say the standard prayers over and over until Peter told me I said enough prayers. I was never taught, nor did not know the truth while I was growing up.

I also thought I might be a Christian, but I was never really sure that there really was a God and what I really was. I was later to be shown the truth by God in his word the Bible. I now know for a fact now that purgatory cannot exist. God requires the shedding of blood for atonement of sin. Nowhere throughout the entire Bible does God state atonement for sin can be made by prayer or by numbers of repeated prayers, or by a priest of any denomination. Without the shedding of blood there is no atonement for sin in God's eyes. In the Old Testament the shedding of blood involved the sacrifice of certain unblemished animals. This was only meant as a temporary solution, as "one" and only "one" future "human" sacrifice was required. When Jesus died on the Cross He was this sacrifice. He is known as the sacrificial lamb. Jesus' death was for atonement of all confessed sin, past, present and future for all true believers. If there was such a place as purgatory; then Jesus did not die for all sin. The Roman Catholic Church is nullifying what Jesus actually did for man.

This is a major contradiction and hypocritical to what is taught throughout the Bible, even the Roman Catholic edition. The only purgatory that could is exist is life as we know it here on earth, but if that were true then Jesus still did not die for "all of our confessed sins." The Bible "does" address the confession and repentance of sin as a requirement set by God. Not the confession to a human being that is standing in for God, but a of sin by the individual to God. When we commit a [sin we ulti]mately sin against God. The Bible does address the [issue when] we wrong someone. We are to confess the offense to the offended party and ask for their forgiveness.

I was also told by the Roman Catholic Church that the Apostle Peter founded the Roman Catholic Church as proof it was the only true religion. I also learned later that this

is a twist of the truth. Peter was totally Jewish not Roman Catholic, and Jesus stated that Peter (which means the rock) was to be the foundation for God's church. The church that was started by Peter and the other apostles was comprised primarily of Jewish believers, not Roman Catholics. Peter headed up the greater Jerusalem crusade, assisted by John, Stephen and Phillip. The Church at the time was then known as "the followers of Jesus." The Roman Catholic Church came along later after the true Church was formed by Peter.

It was Peter who first brought the news of Jesus to "the gentiles." The gentiles were all human beings that were not of Jewish ancestry. This can all be verified in history and in the Bible, even within the Roman Catholic edition of the Bible. The first gentile that converted to becoming a follower of Jesus can be found in reading Acts 10 of the Bible. This gentile convert was a Roman Centurion who resided in Caesarea, a location far from Rome or even Italy for that matter. Peter explains the gentile conversion in Acts 11. The first and true church or followers of Jesus were called "Christians," not Roman Catholics. This happened in Antioch, not in Rome or Italy. This also happened with Barnabas and Paul's mission trip not Peter's (note: Acts 11:25 NIV).

The word "Catholic" simply means one church. All of the true God chosen "Christians," not all of the members within the Roman Catholic, Eastern Orthodox, Jewish, and Protestant organizations, belong to this "one true church": the true church of the followers of Jesus. If you read Revelations chapters 2 and 3 you will note seven churches. All of these churches belong to the "One true church of Jesus." The above noted churches are all branches of the one true church.

I was also taught by the Roman Catholic Church that the priests were God's holy representatives and I must reverence them and call them Father. The Pope is the addressed as the most Holy Father. The Pope is referred to by the members of the Roman Catholic Church as God's personal most holy representative here on earth. This is shown in scripture as something that God forbids as noted in the book of Matthew, chapter 23 (NIV). In the Eastern Orthodox Church it's the priests and the Bishop of the Orthodox Church who are given this reverence.

The Pope, the Bishops, Cardinals and Priests are similar in most every way to the High Priest, Pharisees and Sadducees of the Jewish faith at the time of the ministry of Jesus on earth. Jesus describes them all very well in the book of Matthew chapter 23 (NIV). His description of the Pharisees also accurately fits the Priests of today and Jesus addresses this. The correlation between the current day Priests and the Pharisees is clearly shown. Many people miss this passage in the Bible or do not understand what Jesus is taking about. The Priests, Bishops, Cardinals and the Pope are believed to have a higher calling by the lay people of the church. The Pope, Cardinals, Bishops or priests of any denomination are only human beings. They cannot save themselves, let alone save any one else. Only God can save. The Priests themselves along with the lay people place the Priests, Bishops, Cardinals and the Pope on a pedestal of reverence. This is strictly a "man made" not "God made" rule, and is contrary to the Bible and teachings of Jesus. Jesus knew that to pay reverence to simple priests and denote these people with the title "Father" was going to create a major problem in the future. Study and ponder Matthew 23.

Jesus is precise in his prophecy concerning the future events noted in Matthew. No one at the time that Jesus spoke these words was revered and given the title "Father" except in reference to God alone. Yet Jesus, being God and seeing all time as present, gave us a stern and specific warning in Matthew 23:9 (NIV), "Do not call anyone on earth 'Father.'" This passage can also be found in the Roman Catholic and Orthodox editions of the Bible. Jesus was not referring or talking about our paternal fathers in this warning, as it also states in the Bible that we are to honor our mother and father, and this would be contradictory. Only God, who can see all time in the same moment, would know about Priests being called Father and the similarity of the Pharisees and Priests that would take place in the future. This is just another outstanding proof that Jesus is God. In this passage of the Bible Jesus was referring that we are not to give the unmerited honor bestowed on the priests and church leaders. We disobey the command of Jesus when we bestow the title of "Father" to any human being other than our paternal parent. To reverence any Priest or church leader this way is hypocritical to Christianity and the word of God as stated in the Bible. Ring kissing, bowing or worshipping belongs to God alone. Jesus sternly warns us not to place people on pedestals. Only God belongs on that pedestal. People are frail, flawed and definitely not sinless. God is not. God is infinitely so much more than any mere human.

God also states in the Bible what is done in darkness will be brought to light. We are just learning about the rapes of young boys done by priests that have destroyed so many lives. It is not just priests either; it is any pastor, teacher or human that we place our faith in or put in position of authority or trust. You read about my experience in the military. It wasn't much different and I can well imagine it continues to others to this day. Our faith and trust can only be placed in God alone. If we put our faith and trust in any human, our faith and trust is destroyed when a human lets us down. Jesus stated that we are to look at all true Christians as brothers, sisters, fellow servants, fellow ambassadors, fellow saints and as children of God; all of us are on the same level. We are to respect each other as Christians. The monks are addressed as Brothers and the nuns are addressed as Sisters. Calling a fellow Christian Brother or Sister is correct per the teachings of Jesus as noted in the Bible. Per the Roman Catholic organization only certain people were destined for Sainthood. The Roman Catholic Church would decide who had this high honor. Per God's word in the Bible, "all" true Christians are considered Saints. God decides man's heart and those who are his truly chosen. I have met many people, priests, nuns, rabbi's and pastors who claim to be Christians and are not. I have also met many teachers, rabbi's, and pastors who claim to be right and claim to know God but do not, and they lead many astray. The opposite is also true.

It always had bothered me when I would witness what the priests were doing back when I was younger. What they did never lined up with what they were preaching. If they were God's holy representatives they showed a very poor example. The priests and nuns were abusive. They would hit us kids or would throw a kid around a room without a blink of an eye. If that's what God is like I did not want anything to do with him. Their conduct sure didn't show any loving God to me. Growing up I remember wondering why a certain priest would always be found alone at different attractive housewives homes while the husbands were away at work. I also remember walking into the house of a close friend of our family. I announced myself but no one answered me. I heard this moaning coming out of the bedroom. I thought someone was hurt and went to investigate. What I found was a scantily dressed housewife giving oral sex to this certain priest. I ran out of the house in a hurry and ran home. The priest caught up to me before I reached my house. He gave me this lame explanation about how what I had witnessed was a Holy Sacrament and this woman was receiving special dispensation. I knew what oral sex was.

This priest went on to tell me if I told anyone about what I saw it would be a mortal sin and I would be doomed to hell. What a bunch of baloney!

There was also another priest who paid a little bit too much attention to all the young girls. He had to leave the priesthood when he got a seventeen year old girl pregnant. I also wondered why a lot of priests and nuns always smelled like booze. The witness they showed me eventually drove me away from the Roman Catholic religion. That's why I stated earlier that I never got to know God here. I only knew of him. I also thank God that I never became an altar boy.

If you want to find out factually where the Roman Catholic Church started you really need to check out its history. The Roman Catholic Church started out spreading the good news and teachings of Jesus. This was the first love of the Roman Catholic Church, its roots and its foundation. It has changed over the years and became an organization that has more to do with politics, structure, control, political appointments, innocent bloodshed, money, nobility, pompous ceremony, scandal and payoffs. Its past isn't pretty and quite a lot of atrocities were done in the name of the Roman Catholic Church. It can be further described as a nicely made white coffin. It looks attractive on the outside, but on the inside it is full of dead man's bones. Hopefully with the help of the true believers within the organization it will return to its roots and first love.

I know there must be some form of structure, as well as accountability, or there would most likely be a lot of new cults cropping up lead by strong personalities that impose their own personal agenda. This is where the Bible is so crucial as the foundation, especially the teachings of Jesus. I challenge you to simply check out the "real facts" for yourself. It will require your personal investigation of the Bible and history. You might even find out about the crusades. The war campaigns were originally sent against the Muslims nations to advance Catholicism and included the butchering of innocent women, children, Jews as well as other Christians. How anyone would believe that forcing any religion down someone's throat would ever be accepted with an open heart is ludicrous. It's no wonder why Muslims or Jews for that matter do not take kindly to Christians. Don't be lazy, check it all out. Do not simply ask a priest because chances are that you will not find the truth.

The Truth

Chapter 26

Taking the words of God out of context, or twisting the words, deleting passages or misapplying what is being conveyed distorts the Bible and the message the Bible is conveying is lost. Again I state that God clearly warns us not to do any of this. Revelations 22:18 and 19 strictly applies to every church whether they are Christian based or not. Whether we choose to believe it or not, God is the only judge. Martin Luther tried to wake up the world back in 1517 with the Protestant Reformation with a call to return to the teachings of the Bible.

The Bible is the most important book anyone can own. In a way it is like a puzzle where different parts fit with other parts. If something within the Bible appears to be contradictory the problem is not with the Bible; the problem lies in our understanding of the Bible. For instance: Jesus made the statement, "If you destroy this temple I will raise it up again within three days." The people thought Jesus was referring to the Jewish Temple, the actual building. But Jesus was referring to and calling his body a temple, a temple that housed the Spirit of God, which was crucified and destroyed. His body arose from the grave within three days after His crucifixion.

The Bible is the key to finding the greatest treasure mankind will ever know: everlasting life in a place where there is no sorrow. A place where there is only joy and happiness. If you don't understand a portion of the Bible you just have to ask God to help you understand it. God will guide you and you will find a relationship with Him. Jesus is God. Jesus is the foundation, the corner stone of the Christian Church and the only way to find a relationship with the true God. The Bible contains God's breathed word and what He expects of his church. His church is not a building or organization. His church is made up of the people He dwells in. The people are His temple.

There is an inner core of people within all of the mainline Roman, Orthodox, Protestant, and Jewish Churches that are "true followers of Christ" or true chosen believers that are true "Christians." This inner core is made up of priests, nuns, rabbis and lay people. These believers belong to the true "Catholic" or "one Christian Church" of Jesus that is made up the true believers of all the various Christian organizations. If you are one of the truly chosen, it is your obligation as a Christian to hold whatever "organization" you are a member of accountable to the word of God found in the Bible. I have learned all of what I am conveying over many years through diligent effort in seeking God. Now I want to continue bringing the reader back to an earlier time in my life to demonstrate how God worked on me and molded me over time by placing experiences and people in my life.

Feeding the Seed

Chapter 27

It was now June 1977. We sold our house in Bridgewater and had bought a handy man special house in Braintree, Massachusetts. Braintree is about ten miles south of downtown Boston. The house we bought was covered in vines. It was only shingled on the front of the house and on one side. The garage was falling down and there was a big hole in the roof. The house had been abandoned and neglected for many years. A motorcycle gang was occupying the house as a hang out. There was human waste all over the place. Someone had used the corner of the living room as a fireplace. The kitchen had a huge hole in the middle of the floor. Basically, like me, it was a dump. But it was all we could afford. This was going to be a major challenge. I didn't have a clue how to fix a house, but I was to become a fast learner. I now had a desire to learn, a desire I never had in school. I learned about everything that had to do with building houses. I had a desire to start from the dirt up and learn it all. Excavation, site preparation, foundation, framing, siding, roofing, plumbing, electrical, insulation, and drywall were all fascinating to me. When I wasn't working on my house I was working with some friends in the trades, learning while I helped. In turn I learned all of the trades. This was something my father could never do. He knew books, but he could not fix simple things around the house, much less anything complex.

Our car at the time was a 1960 Dodge Valiant. It had a rebuilt slant six engine and my friend helped me put in a rebuilt 3 speed transmission. I fixed most of the dents and rust with fiberglass filler and then hand painted it with this chestnut brown paint someone had given me. It wasn't pretty, but it worked. It would get us from point A to Point B. The car didn't have seat belts and the rear floor had rotted out. I had screwed in a piece of sheet metal to cover a big hole in the floor.

I remember taking the twins out to the store one day. This was before mandatory seat belt laws. Danielle would at least sit in the seat; not so with Dee. Dee had to be bouncing all over the place. Well, this time she bounced right through the sheet metal I had put on the floor. Thank God I was going up hill and not traveling fast. She managed to just grab the head rest in the nick of time before she would have been pulled under the car. There was another time when Dee kept playing with the door handle; the next thing we knew she was half hanging out the door and half in the car as we were driving down the road. This was before child proof door locks. I thanked God that his angels were out there watching over us.

In 1979 our lives started to change for the better. Shortly after Adriana was born I had received a letter offering me a job in downtown Boston with the post office as an LSM operator. LSM means Letter Sorting Machine. I had to take a test and if I passed I would be hired. I passed, thank God. To be a LSM operator I had to be able to look at a letter as it passes in front of me on a conveyer belt. I had to read the letter, find the zip code and punch in the corresponding post office regional center code that it corresponded to in one second. It's a lot harder to do than it sounds and not many people can do it. I also had to be 98% correct. I was constantly checked for accuracy. If I wasn't accurate I would fall under the three strikes you're out rule.

Although I had had this prior experience in meeting God in my back yard, I was not instantly changed into a Holy Roller. I still had a lot of my old bad habits. I could not handle the prescription drugs in coping with my PTSD. Instead of turning to God for help with my PTSD and problems, I eventually turned to street drugs to replace the prescription drugs that did not work for me. I was no stranger to my drug of choice. Marijuana, cannabis, Mary Jane, reefer, weed, bone, joint, pot, whatever you want to call it. In time I eventually did experiment with a number of other street drugs. I snorted and freebased cocaine, tried LSD, mescaline, speed, crystal meth, Quaaludes, and knew if I didn't stop crack and heroin were only a stepping stone away. I had a bad trip one night on mescaline and that snapped me away from everything but the pot. I found I could function on marijuana so I stayed with it. It was part of my life almost every day. It was the only thing that helped me. All I can say is everyone's chemistry is different. Different drugs affect everyone differently. I can't handle alcohol or different kinds of medicines. Pot seemed to affect me differently than it did to others that smoke it.

I strongly believe there is a medical use for marijuana and more research needs to be done. My problem was that marijuana was illegal. For me, marijuana took away the inner rage from the physiological damage in my head done from the assault in the military. I was able to sleep without the nightmares, I wasn't getting ulcers, I wasn't having my continuous problem with acid reflux, my stomach was not twisted up in knots anymore and I did not have all the side effects I had with all of the prescribed medications.

I have not smoked or used marijuana for over 15 years now as I felt convicted by my family as a Christian to stop. Mainly, I felt it would hurt my witness for God, even though there is nothing in the Bible that directly states "Thou shall not smoke the weed!" I went back to prescribed medicines, though none have worked to date and all of the medicines have the unwanted side effects. I also don't know what long term effects they will have on me. But I am hanging in there. I have brought the situation to God and I was given the same answer as the Apostle Paul. Simply put, his grace is sufficient for me.

I also found, as did others, that I could do this particular post office job better being stoned. I know, I know, people, doctors, whoever will argue to the contrary. But in my case I was constantly tested for accuracy. I messed up constantly when I was straight and when I was stoned I would get perfect scores. With this particular job the less you concentrated the better you could do the job. If you thought about what you were doing you wasted precious fractions of seconds and would mess up. You had to be in a self-hypnotic state to do this job. That's why most of the people that did this job the best, were stoned. Not only were most of us stoned, but we also had headphones on that were tuned to our favorite station, mainly rock and roll. It made for a rhythm that worked. Since we all had similar interests, we all hung out together for breaks and lunch. Quite often we would make sure we were off government property to get further experienced with Mary Jane during our lunch breaks. It had all the ingredients for a life that should have headed away from God. But God does the miraculous. Once he planted that seed in me, I was his. He would bring me around in his time and change me. God accepts you as you are, baggage and all.

    It would be around 1:00 or 2:00 in the morning when I would leave work. I had a half hour drive home every night. I would light up a joint and drive. My car radio only had one station which is quite a coincidence. It was WEEZ 590 on the AM dial. It was a Christian broadcasting station. Since I was stoned I was in my happy place, relaxed without the inner rage gnawing at me. I started to listen to the radio program just to hear something. I know now what I didn't know then: that the seed that God had planted in me was now being fed. The station played certain regular programs, mostly radio preachers. I started to really get into the programs. I found myself actually looking forward to hear more and more. When I arrived home I would even stay up another hour or so just listening. I had never heard any of this information before, yet it could have been easily found if I had only read the Bible. So hearing all of this led me to deeply check out the Bible on my own. I got copies of all different types of Bibles. The Roman Catholic version, the Orthodox Catholic version, the King James versions, both old and revised, the NIV, the NIrV and the living Bible; I had copies of them all. They were my treasured possessions, but I eventually gave most of them to people I eventually witnessed to, as they would not have a Bible. I would listen to the Christian broadcasting station every chance I could, at least an hour to four or five hours a day. I would switch my headset in work from rock and roll to this Christian radio station. I started reading and cross referencing using all the Bibles I had.

I was also finding out what prayer meant. It was so enjoyable to see God responding to my prayers. I was learning how to talk to God and learning to wait and see His reply. I was developing my relationship with God. I was learning to trust God. I was growing in my faith, learning to put all my trust in him. In all of this I found God personally involved in my life. I would talk to Him every chance I could, making sure He was first on my list. I wouldn't make a move without Him. My mind was constantly on God during all of this. I wondered more and more about Him. I was getting to know Him and recognize His hand, His involvement, in everything. I was also seeing God getting involved with me and my personal life even though I was still a sinner.

The Accident

Chapter 28

I did not know it at the time, but my faith and trust in God was about to be tested. It was now December and Christmas was right around the corner. My wife, Adri and I were off to buy Christmas presents. It was around 1:00 in the afternoon. It was a sunny day. I had just come off the expressway and was waiting in a line of traffic stopped at a red light in front of me. Then when we least expected it this car came up from behind us without stopping! I turned out that this guy had had a liquid lunch and he didn't notice the traffic had stopped in front of him. He slammed into the rear of my car, pushing it with tremendous force into a four car chain reaction. He had to be traveling at least 30 to 40 miles an hour.

My car was crushed like an accordion, and so were two other cars in front of me. My wife was holding my daughter Adriana on her lap in the front seat. Seat belts were not mandatory then. Adriana was only two years old and was bundled up in a snow suit covered from head to toe. If she had been in the back seat she most likely would not have survived. She was completely unharmed, which was a miracle. My wife's knee was stuck in the dashboard, and the fuse-holding prongs of the fuse box were stuck in her knee. As for me, I felt funny all over but I didn't really feel hurt. I guess I was in shock. In fact, I didn't totally realize it at the time, but I wasn't feeling anything at all. I was so concerned about my wife and child.

The jerk that hit us could hardly stand up he was so drunk. My daughter was checked out and she was fine. My wife refused to go the hospital to be checked out. I thought I was just so shook up and I just wanted to go home and lie down.

A few hours later I remember waking up and not feeling right. I was having difficulty breathing. My body was tingling all over like when your leg falls asleep. My legs and the lower portion of my body were numb. It felt as though I was full of ants and they were crawling inside the lower part of my body. This was mixed with pain in the upper areas of my body that were not so numb. This would increase and decrease as I would I move my neck around. My wife wanted to call for an ambulance, but being stubborn, I said lets just get in the car and drive to the hospital ourselves. I was still able to walk, but my legs and arms now were feeling like lead weights. They took x-rays, put my neck in a collar and paged the doctor on call.

When the doctor finally arrived he seemed to be put out to be called in the middle of the night. He didn't perform a thorough exam on me. He didn't even look at the x-rays. He just assumed this was going to be the typical back or neck injury insurance scam. He just looked at me and said I was fine; I just must have pulled a muscle. He told me to go home and take an aspirin and I would be fine in the morning. He didn't even ask me about my symptoms or what I was feeling; or more correctly not feeling. So, my wife and I went home.

As we were pulling into to our driveway, this same doctor pulled up, driving like a maniac. He got out of his car and ran over to me. He kept apologizing while at the same time telling me not to move. He had finally woken up and checked out the x-rays. My cervical (neck) spine was dislocated in four places and was pressed against and bending my spinal cord. I was told my spinal cord was a millimeter from being severed. I was not going to settle for his opinion, as I thought he was insane.

I sought out numerous "other" opinions from all of Boston's finest doctors and hospitals. By the fifth opinion, I kept being told the same thing, even with repetitive x-rays. All of the doctors that saw me were totally amazed that I was even alive, let alone not completely paralyzed from the neck down. They could not believe that I was standing in front of them and functioning. Traction, the neck brace and time were the only recommend treatment by all of the doctors at the various hospitals. They all told me the same thing. In my case, neck fusion was not a good option. I was told at the time, I would have only a 25 percent chance of surviving the operation. There was even a greater risk that if I did manage to survive the operation I would most likely be paralyzed from the neck down. The doctors also told me that as I aged I would most likely have a problem with arthritis in my neck. I was told that I would have to make a major adjustment on my lifestyle.

As it turns, out they were more than right. Not only did I get the arthritis, but I also got interior bone spurs that eventually penetrated my spinal cord. I'll get into this a little later in the book. I could sit around and cry "poor me." I guess I could even blame and get mad at God. I thought I was developing a good relationship with God and now this. What was happing to me? I guess I could also fold the cards I was dealt and check out of this world. Or I could accept what happened, adjust and play the cards I was dealt.

What I learned is that it was something that God needed me to go through. It was a test and I eventually made it through the test. My relationship with God was made even stronger as I refused to lose my faith and continued trust in him to see me through this nightmare. I was learning to lean on God for the strength I needed to get me through this. The medical term for what happened to me in the accident was called an interior sublexation of the cervical spine in C2 through C6. What I found I had is something similar to putting kinks in hose. The spinal cord is the hose containing all of the nerves that run from the brain at C1 down the spinal cord and then throughout all the various parts of the body.

If a hose, even an ordinary garden hose, has fluid or water passing through it and pressure is put on the hose, or the hose is bent, or if there is a kink in the hose, the fluid either stops or comes out in a wild spray. In my case, my neck was unstable and how I moved determined how much and where pressure was placed on the spinal cord containing the nerve trunk. I would receive pain or total numbness in various parts of my body. I found that this was worse when I try to sleep because I moved around in my sleep and would often wake up in excruciating pain even when I wore the neck brace. Sometimes the neck brace would even make things worse. I was learning what I could do and what not to do. The wrong move could put me in severe pain for days to weeks. In time my symptoms became worse. Sometimes it would feel as though my hands were hit and crushed by a sledge hammer; sometimes it felt like a part of my body was severed. If you looked at me from the outside, I looked like I was in good shape.

The insurance company of the jerk that hit me wanted to offer me $28,000 to forget the whole thing and let them off the hook. My injury was permanent and I would be in pain from this injury the rest of my life. What they offered wouldn't even pay the current medical expenses, let alone any of the other financial problems this caused. I had to hire a lawyer. Before I could go back to work at the post office I had to see the post office doctor for a physical. I begged him to let me pass, but he would only say that he was sorry, he could not do it. He told me that if I could find another doctor that would sign a report guaranteeing that I was healed of my injury he would let me come back to work. He knew that wouldn't happen. I could not find a doctor that would say I was cured, or even state that I would not get worse, as they would be worried that they may be sued for malpractice. So instead of letting me come back to work, the post office gave me a small plaque, a hand shake, a small pension and a farewell.

I didn't know what I was going to do. Any job would require a physical or release of my medical records and they would refuse to hire me. Wherever I went I would be told the same old story. They could not take on the responsibility of hiring me knowing I would most likely get worse. I was in a real tough situation; a situation that I could only get through with God's help. The next few years were a major struggle.

The Struggle

Chapter 29

Getting into court takes years and you don't receive any money while you wait. So, not being able to get a regular job, I went back to college again. I went to Boston State College in a neck collar and graduated in the last class of Boston State before it was merged with the University of Massachusetts. Being a veteran and a resident of the state, my tuition was free under the GI bill. I was also given a check for going to school under veterans' benefits. I also applied for aid under the Massachusetts Veterans Services to pay my mortgage until I could get things straightened out with the insurance company. The state veterans' service office had me sign an agreement stating that they would get paid back when I received my insurance settlement from the accident. I also got the lawyer to send out agreements for payment to my debtors and doctors when my case was settled. We were also eligible for food stamps. It was a very humbling experience. Except for my neck collar, I "looked" just as healthy as everyone else. We had a junk box for a car, but it worked. It was a hard time; we were just barely getting by. It was so frustrating. I was doing everything and anything I could. I just had to hang in there and trust God to get us through.

It's sad how people look down on others when they're poor without knowing their whole situation. I remember going grocery shopping with my wife. When my wife went to pay for the groceries with the food stamps the female cashier immediately had an attitude change. The cashier made sure that my wife, me and all the people standing in line, heard and knew of her "low tolerance of people like us." The cashier with a disgusted look on her face snorted, "Lady that's all you have? I don't see why we have to wait on you people anyway." She then made reference that we should go somewhere else to do our shopping. I more embarrassed for my wife; none of this was our fault. I was getting a life education I will never forget.

I know what it is like to be poor and how bad some people treat you when you're poor. I decided then that I was going to get us out of this mess somehow. Ag and I survived and we were strengthened in our faith by the whole ordeal. I have always carried the memory of all we went through. It was from this experience that Ag and I would later start up and operate the Braintree Community Food Pantry. This pantry serves all of the less fortunate in our community. We don't judge anyone. Everyone of any race, social standing or religious belief is welcomed. We just help anyone in need.

I stayed in college, concentrating my study on math, science, psychology and business in seeking a bachelor's degree. I eventually received my bachelor's degree. Business Management was my major and Psychology was my minor. I went further in my college studies and received my Massachusetts teaching certification for math and earth science as well as business subjects.

It took me three years to get into court. All that time without a paycheck, no money from the insurance companies and no money from our lawyer. We survived totally relying on God to get us through. When we got into court the jerk that hit me took the stand. He had a matter of fact, but in no way apologetic attitude. He admitted that he didn't realize the traffic had stopped and that's why he hit us. We also learned that he was the "kept" companion of a well-known and well-connected founder of a large hardware and lumber chain. By the time the jury went in to deliberate the insurance company decided to offer me $150,000 to settle the case. My lawyer advised me not to accept the offer and to stay with the jury.

The jury came back with a guilty verdict and felt $500,000 was a fair settlement. The judge, whom I firmly believe was bought and paid for, stated the amount seemed excessive and decided $150,000 was more appropriate. I wonder how he came up with that figure? It ended my case right there. I was told by my lawyer that there could be no appeal. The lawyer received $50,000, the debtors received $75,000 and I received $25,000. I still had my injury, no job, PTSD and had no idea what I was going to do. I knew $25,000 was not going to get us through the rest of our lives. I did not find any justice in the courtroom. I still would not give up my faith in God. I had no place else to turn. I just had to hang on and hang in there with God as my guide.

In college I found math and science interesting and for me it was easy to comprehend. I found out later I was successful in tutoring children and adults who never could understand it. After receiving my college degree and teacher certification, I tried to get a full-time permanent teaching position. Full-time teaching positions within an hour commute of my home were scarce. Ag refused to move. The rare full-time positions that did open up were mostly filled by "who you know" not, "what you know" individuals. When I would luck out and almost get a full-time teaching position my medical records cropped up and I would lose out. Time went on and I could only get temporary teaching positions. I didn't have any clout so I thought God must have something else in mind for me. So I went back to school and I received my real estate brokers license. I went to work in the office of a friend of my mother's. I did quite well. I pulled us out of the hole and then some. I worked 80 hours a week when I had to. Keeping my family in mind and all that we had gone through was a strong motivator.

A Miracle

Chapter 30

It was now 1982 and "we" were pregnant again. I just kept thinking we were going to have another daughter. As Ag was getting bigger, we learned that she had a fibroid growing in her that was three times bigger than the baby. All the doctors were telling us that Ag would most likely miscarriage and lose the baby. She was about seven months into the pregnancy and now the fibroid was massive. But for some reason we both felt peaceful inside and knew that everything was going to be okay.

Around this same time my younger sister Lori, who was very sick, was getting worse. Lori had two kidney transplants with two of my brothers and both transplants failed. We had heard that this priest Father Diorio was going to be in an area about two hours' drive from us. This priest supposedly had a healing gift from God. I did trust in God and who ever he worked through was okay with me. I figured it couldn't hurt and maybe my sister could be healed. Ag and I took my sister hoping for a miracle. When we were about 3 miles from where this priest was going to be we saw cars all lined up on the side of the road with no place left to park. There was also no way my sister could walk that far, so I prayed to Jesus asking him for his help. I kept driving and as I was approaching the entrance preparing to go past it a car just pulled out of a parking space in front of me. I pulled in and parked. "Wow, that was weird," I thought.

There was a hill beside us with a path that we had to use to get to where the priest would be. As we approached the top of the hill we saw thousands of people all sitting in a circle up around the hill that surrounded this open church in the center. There was a podium and some benches in this open church area. Around this area was a fence with a gate. I saw this really big guy standing at the gate. I thought there was no hope now as there was nowhere to even sit. But then, as I looked down toward the podium this big guy seemed to be pointing at me and waving me to come forward. I thought he must be pointing to someone else, as he was pretty far away and there were a lot of people, but they were all sitting and I was standing. I pointed at myself while looking at him and he waved again. This was really weird, I thought.

So Ag, my sister and I made our way down the hill through all the people to this guy. When I reached him he opened the gate and told me to follow him. It was about the third row from the front of the podium and he told us to sit. We did. You tell me what that was all about! When I turned to see the big guy again he was nowhere to be found. Then this priest came out and was saying a "mass." He started walking around touching people and praying over them. There was a lot of commotion and people were claiming to be healed and falling down. Then he started to walk towards us. I was praying to beat the band. I wasn't paying much attention to the priest, when suddenly I looked up as he was standing beside me tapping me on the shoulder. I tried to get his focus on my sister but he shook his head no and told me and my wife to stand up. He then prayed over us and moved on. I didn't know what that was all about, and I was really upset that my sister was not the one he prayed over.

Ag was having weekly ultrasounds done in keeping track of the fibroid and the baby. A few days after seeing this priest we were to have another ultrasound done and a determination was going to be made as they felt the baby was in danger and they may have to take the baby prematurely. When they took the ultrasound this time they found that the fibroid was completely gone. It is weird, but God still does miracles.

Our Son Marc

Chapter 31

Girls, women, females have always fascinated me, ever since I was very young. In fact, nothing can turn my head faster than a woman. Maybe it's the Italian in me. I used to think it would be great if I had several daughters. When I grew older it would be wonderful to be surrounded by beautiful women that loved me. I didn't know that God was going to give me this dream. What I found out was that living with girls as they grew up was not a simple thing or as wonderful as I had imagined.

I found that girls are very hard to figure out. They seem to work more on emotion than logic. Raising them along with their strange habits was a major struggle for me. There were always pantyhose and unmentionable items hanging in the bathroom that I would have to wade through when I wanted to take a shower or use the toilet. Girls can also occupy a bathroom for hours, and with them use of the bathroom is always an emergency. They seem to shower and change clothes twenty times a day. They can cry at anything you say. When you try to get them to stop crying you end up saying something that makes them cry even more. Girls love to shop. When they shop, they don't just go in, get the item they came for and leave as most males do. No, not girls, they love to meander through stores like butterflies. They are attracted to the most ridiculous things that males wouldn't give a second look at.

As my girls grew, so did my headaches. I now had to worry

about the boys that were taking an interest in my girls. I know how guys think and they better not think that way around my girls. It's a real struggle raising three girls. Now I figured we would be having four girls and even more headaches.

The time had finally arrived for my wife to deliver or fourth child. Again it was to be by C section. As I went with my wife down to the operating room a nurse met us. She wanted to know why I wasn't ready.

"Ready for what?" I asked.

"Aren't you going to come in and watch the delivery of your baby?"

I said, "You're kidding, right?"

She wasn't kidding and I wasn't sure I would be able to handle it. Then she said, "It's okay, you're probably afraid and we don't need anyone fainting in there during this."

That did it for me. "I'm not afraid of anything. What do I have to do?" I said.

They suited me up while they prepared my wife and then brought me into the room. I will never, ever forget that day. The memories it holds for me are as fresh today as they were then. My wife had a small curtain that was set up just under her chin so that she could not see what was happening from the neck down. There was a stool for me there allowing me to see both sides of the curtain. Here she was talking to me and asking me questions while on the other side of the curtain they had cut and completely exposed the inside of her stomach. It was freaky, like something out of a horror movie. For a second I even thought I was in a butcher shop. The room was dimly lit with soft lighting. However, bright lights were focused on the area where the doctors were working on my wife. It was all like being in a dream. Then the doctor reached into my wife's open exposed stomach, and pulled out, among other things, this little baby boy. The cord was still attached and he was covered with blood. The doctor put this clip on the cord and asked if I would like the honor of cutting the cord. I couldn't believe this was all really happening. My head was swimming as I took it all in and then reality struck me. The baby was a boy, not another girl but a boy, I have a son!

The doctor handed the baby to the nurses as they had a little wash station where they cleaned him up. They sucked out the mucus from his nose and mouth, they got his footprints and then they gave him a shot in his leg. He came alive when they gave him that shot. Man, could he scream. The placenta had stopped working and he had lost most of his weight. He looked more like a blood hound than a boy with the loose skin hanging off him. But he was okay and he was mine, my son, Marc! He was now wrapped in blanket as I brought him over to see his mother before they put her out. She thought he looked like ET. She also said he was one ugly baby. The tears of our joy just kept flowing.

Growing up, as you can probably imagine, he was spoiled. He never gave his mother or me any problems growing up. He also has his mother's tender heart. When he was a boy he was a lot like Adri and always had me carry him around or needed to be on my lap. Now that he is grown into a man he says I drive him crazy. He is getting married next August to a beautiful woman that he has known since they were both kids. Her name is Amanda. I see a lot of my wife in Amanda. Children flock to Amanda like they do to my Adri. Children instinctively know who has a tender heart. Marc always told me even when Amanda was just a teenager dating other boys that she was the only girl for him. His friends and I joked about it once and Marc told us to just wait and see; Amanda will come around. I guess he was right.

Our Son John

Chapter 32

I was doing well in real estate and my girls were all grown by 1993. At this time Ag ("the walking heart") approached me with a zinger. She had read a news article about this severely abused five year old boy. She had called the social service office to get more information about him without telling me first. She told me his story and it's hard to believe a five year old could have gone through what this kid went through. Ag wanted to take in this child.

Our children were grown up and I was looking forward to the easier years, not taking in somebody else's headache! But, Ag still wanted to take in this child. I told her it was a big mistake and I did not want to do it, but this woman knows how to break me down. So I finally gave in and agreed to try it only on a temporary basis. I figured it was a fad she had to get out of her system, sort of like girls and Barbie dolls. I figured a week with this kid and it would be out of her system.

She went and did what she had to do and the next thing I know I have this little blonde haired, blue eyed little boy calling me, "Big daddy." Well, it lasted longer than a week. For the first 30 days I thought the Antichrist was living with us. His name is John. John made Dennis the Menace look like an angel. John had had a nervous breakdown before we took on temporary guardianship. John had PTSD, a huge inferiority complex and a major problem with stuttering. Every day he was either zoning out or taking fits of rage. Everything we said, he responded by contradicting us. He always gave us a struggle and a hard time. Every night he would have night rages. He broke every window in the house and all the glass in the windows of the French doors. He would topple the furniture, break the drawers, slam into doors, kick and scream like a wild animal and run away. When he was outside he would throw anything or kick things at the house and windows. He even broke off sections of the vinyl siding on the exterior of the house.

I understood what this child went through and my heart wept for him. For his protection I cannot reveal his past; the reader will just have to imagine the worst and John's experience went beyond that. I can say that no child, no human being, nor any animal should have been treated as he was. He was more than we bargained for. I didn't know who was more nuts, this kid or us for taking him. I kept pleading with Ag, please send this kid back, he's too much to handle. Even though I strongly felt he was more than my wife or I could handle, my wife wouldn't give in. She is one stubborn Albanian woman. When he was out of control she would wrap her arms around him and hang on to him. All the while she would gently rock him while softly telling him, "It's okay, John. You're okay, you're okay now." She would melt me. She never gave up on him and I witnessed her love turn this kid around.

His real mother is still alive. The state of Massachusetts had temporarily taken away her parental rights. No one really knows who his real father is. The mother had had a number of partners and a long history of personal and drug abuse. There is a name registered on his birth certificate who the mother claims is John's father, but that individual claims he is not the father. The mother had two other children, both of which were also taken away by the state. All of the children have different fathers. John had been placed in specialized foster care. He was in the foster care program for children with serious psychological and emotional problems. The children placed in this facility most likely would never be chosen for adoption or placement in a normal family setting.

Children like John usually end up spending most of their lives growing up in an institutional setting. They are considered by society as throw away children. My wife, ("the walking heart") was determined not to let this happen to John. He had been with us for several years and yet I thought it wouldn't last a week. Over time, between Ag's care and God's intervention, I witnessed a miracle happening with this child.

The time came when the state was pressuring us to either adopt John or take full guardianship of him. We all came together as a family in pondering a decision on whether we should do what the state wanted or not. It was not easy as John had a lot of baggage due to what other adults had done to him. There was also a very high possibility that serious issues could arise in the future as he got older. The family was split on the decision, three for it and three against it. We all agreed not to go with the adoption as the natural mother was still in the picture and she was threatening a law suit if an adoption was attempted. So now we had to decide whether or not we should take full guardianship of John. I was one of the three votes against the decision to accept guardianship. Since we could not give the state a definite yes before their imposed deadline and I was not inclined to change my mind, they took John out of our home and placed him back in the children's center.

My wife still would not give up and would go to visit John regularly. I refused to go with her. I did not think I should encourage my wife. I had reminded her when we started this process that I only agreed on a temporary arrangement. I never agreed to anything permanent! I felt she was being totally unfair to me about the whole arrangement. I also was being a little selfish and felt that I was entitled to a life. I had struggles of my own I was trying to overcome. I had worked hard, been through a lot and I had raised my children. I was still dealing with the PTSD and my injury on a daily basis. I knew from first hand experience that life is not fair. I also realized that no one out there said it would be. It was most unfortunate what happened to this child. What happened to this child happened from bad choices the child's mother made, not choices made by me.

Even though Ag knew how strongly I felt she still refused to give up. She would come home after visiting this child and just go straight to our room. She would collapse on the bed and weep uncontrollably. After several weeks of this it was more than I could bear. I was losing my wife. She was in mourning for this child as though he were dead. I finally agreed to go and visit him with her, but I made no promises, just a visit. When we showed up at the children's center, the child's adviser told us that John was in the gym. He spent most of his days there, alone, just sitting on the floor in a corner, with his coat over his head. He wouldn't talk to anyone and he would rarely eat. He was withdrawing from life at a fast pace.

When I walked into the room I couldn't believe what I saw. He looked like a stray under nourished dog that was dying. He would not raise his head when I spoke to him. He wouldn't even answer me when I talked to him. I turned to look at my wife only to see her sobbing. I couldn't take anymore. I turned and told her I would meet her in the car. I was still determined to keep my hard heart. We didn't speak at all on the ride home.

When we got home she just went to our room, threw herself on our bed and sobbed. I walked in our room and she turned to me and pleaded. "Please Mark, please." When God dwells within you the seed that he plants surely grows. You can try to cling to your selfish self-centered hard heart, but God will win every time. He takes away that old selfish nature and plants a new one. He shatters and melts hard hearts and replaces them with a heart of love and compassion. The new nature that is given by God is not bent any longer on "what's in it for me." What's in it for me is not what life is about. With God working in this whole ordeal, Ag's prayers and cries were heard. Ag and the boy had succeeded. I couldn't take it anymore. My hard heart was shattered. All this child ever wanted was a forever family. All this child had ever talked about was being a part of a forever family. My heart and my vote were changed. Now the vote was two against and four for it. I changed the decision so that this child would be made a permanent part of our family. One of the two against votes also saw the light as well and changed their vote.

My children thought we should do something special when we told this child of our decision. My children all got together and drew a picture of our family; there was Ag and I, our three girls, my son Marc and next to Marc was now our new son John. Oh yeah, I almost forgot, next to John was "Baby," our miniature dachshund. On the top of the picture the girls wrote the words "Our Forever Family" in big bold letters. They then cut the picture into puzzle pieces. Then it was time to go and reveal our family decision to John.

We had told the state of our decision and they were very excited. We were to meet at the center that evening around 8:00 o'clock. We told them not to let John know of our decision as we wanted to tell him our way. We all went as a family. John's social worker and his adviser met us. We were all in a private room when they sent for John. He saw us all and at first did not want to come in to the room. His head was downcast and I spoke up and told him I was here because I needed his help. I had this puzzle and I couldn't quite figure it out. I asked him if he could help me. He eventually looked up and walked over to the table where I had placed the puzzle pieces. He looked at the pieces and said, "You're kidding right? Even Baby could do this puzzle!"

I said, "Are you going to give me a hard time or are you going to help me?"

"Fine, I'll help," he said.

I had taken the piece of the puzzle that he was drawn on and put it in my pocket. He put the puzzle together and noticed the missing piece. He said, "Something is missing."

I said, "Yes John, that's right. Now, what do you think is missing?"

He noticed the words our forever family right off the bat. Then he studied the picture some more. He said, "Well here's Ag, here's you, this has to be Danielle, this one has to be Deanna, there's Adri and Marc. Oh, I get it! Baby's missing, that's what's missing."

I said, "Yes, John, Baby is missing from the picture! Maybe I just misplaced the missing piece of everyone who is in our forever family picture. Let me see if I left it in my pocket. Why yes, yes, here it is John, this is the missing piece of our forever family." I handed him the missing piece from my pocket and at first he was so proud that it fit, and then he looked and looked some more.

He then saw himself in the picture of "Our Forever Family" and Baby was next to him. At that very moment he looked up and looked straight into my eyes. I saw his tears and heard the cry in his voice as he said to me, "You mean it! Big daddy, do you really mean it!"

"Yes John, I really mean it."

There were a lot of tears on the floor that night and a whole lot of hugging. February 2005 John turned sixteen.

This kid is a natural "chick" magnet for women of all ages. He's the closest thing I've seen to James Dean going. The girls take one look at this kid and melt. The phone doesn't stop from all the girls looking for John and now we're getting into "the driving license stage" of his life. I'm Dad and Ag's Mom to John. We hear from his natural mother every few years after she is straight after going through detox. These times Ag and I feel the mother calls or sends a card mainly motivated out of guilt. John does not want anything to do with her and will not take her call or even look at her cards. He also refuses to have any contact with his step brothers.

A few years ago John tested me, as he often does. I bought a few rolls of the Susan B. Anthony coins and was keeping them to pass out to my grandchildren. I safely keep them in a drawer in my room. This is a place off limits to everyone but me and is acknowledged by everyone in the family. One day my wife and I had gone out to dinner when one of my daughters called. She had stopped by our house as all my children often do and noticed John's backpack was thrown on the floor in the front hallway. Falling out of the backpack and all over the floor were Susan B. Anthony coins. John had gone out with his friends and he must have been in a hurry and just threw the bag down on the floor before he went out the door.

When I arrived home I dumped his backpack out to see what was going on. He probably had close to a hundred dollars worth of these coins in his bag. I put them all back in his backpack and waited for him to come home. When he arrived home I asked him to come into my room so that we could talk. I never raised my voice and talked to him calmly. I asked him if I had always been good to him and always been fair with him.

He said, "Yes."

I asked him if I had ever hit or abused him.

He said, "No."

I asked him if I had ever taken anything of his that did not belong to me.

He said, "No" again.

I then asked him if he was mad at me or if he wanted to hurt me.

He said, "Of course not."

I then said to him, "Didn't I take you into my home, didn't I always treat you as my son, do I always give you money when you ask me to, do I always provide for you, do you have your own room, your own TV, your own stereo, your own X-box, your own computer, your own phone?"

He said, "Yes" to all.

I then asked him, "Then why did you hurt me?" At that point I got his bag and dumped it out. I told him not to say anything to me at that moment. I told him that I wanted him to think about things and we would talk the next day when he came home from school. I remember hating when my parents made me wait for my punishment. I would have rather them shoot me and get it over with right then and there. But no, they had to let it fester in my mind wondering what they were going to do me. Of course, my daughter had sounded the alarm to all of the other siblings and as usual they all had their opinions on what action Dad should have taken. I think their general consensus was that John should be tarred and feathered.

When John came home the next day after school I told him to please come into my office and close the door. I asked him to sit down so that we were eye to eye. I asked him calmly if he thought about yesterday and had he anything he wanted to say. It was quiet for a while and then with his eyes downcast he said, "I did it."

"You did what John?" I asked.

"I took the coins from your drawer," he said.

"John, did they belong to you?" I asked.

"No, they belonged to you," he said.

"Then why did you take them? Why did you steal from me?" I asked.

"A voice told me to do it," he said.

"I see," I said. "Do you think it was a good voice or a good thing to do?" I asked.

His answer was, "No."

"Can you see that I trusted you and you hurt that trust?" I said.

"I didn't mean to hurt you and I'm sorry," he said. His eyes were still downcast and he was crying.

"What do you think I should do John?" I asked.

He said, "I need to be punished."

"Okay, I think your right. How should you be punished, what do you think is fair?" I asked.

He said, "I think you should probably send me back to the center."

I knew it! I knew this was where he was going with all this. I calmly replied, "I see, but I can't do that John. Even if I could send you back I wouldn't do that. You see, when I asked you to be part of our forever family, I meant forever. Good or bad you're, stuck with us and we are stuck with you. We're not ever going to send you back to the center John."

I let him think about what I said for a minute and then I continued. "You know how I always tell you about Jesus? When Jesus accepts us into his family, it's forever John. We all mess up and do the wrong things sometimes. This hurts Jesus in the same way you hurt me. When we do something wrong it usually effects someone else or something else. We all deserve to be punished. God still accepts us even when we have messed up all our lives. If we belong to God's family, he does not throw us out of his family if we do wrong. He will discipline us, but he will also forgive us. We might have to suffer the consequences of our actions, but God doesn't say we are no longer His child. Instead of giving us the real punishment we deserve, Jesus allowed Himself to be into a human body and took this punishment for us when he was brutally tortured and nailed to a cross. He did this for us, because God knows we could not bear the punishment we deserve. God forgives us not because He has to, but because He loves us. We do not deserve what Jesus did for us. What He did for us also allows God to show us His mercy and grace so that we can learn to also follow his example and do the same thing.

"I will give you another example. For what you did I think you should be punished this way: today is Friday, for a full 3 months starting today, you are not allowed to go out anywhere after school or on the weekends. You are not allowed to watch television, no stereo allowed, no walkman, no phone calls, no x-box and no contact with friends. Everyday you will put in two more hours doing school work and chores around the house. What do you think about that punishment John, do you think it is fair?" I asked.

Although he looked a little pale by now, he said that he thought it was a little unfair.

I said, "Good, then that's what your punishment will be." But I wasn't done. Then I said, "Now I am going to teach you what mercy and grace are all about. You deserve the punishment I told you, but I am going to be merciful to you and by not giving you the punishment you deserve. You have to suffer the consequences of what you did and that means I can not trust you the same as I did and you will have to prove to me in time that I will be able to trust you as I did before. Today is Friday, the day that you are to begin your punishment. As I am being merciful, the punishment will not start until Monday and it will end in two weeks. Now I will also show you what grace is all about. I have done most of your punishment for you. So since most of the punishment is done you only have an additional 24 hours of punishment for the consequences of your actions, so now your punishment ends on Tuesday."

Now he was looking into my eyes. His face beamed as he showed his joy. He then just broke down and sobbed saying over and over how sorry he was and how much he loved me. Then I said, "Okay, enough discussion, now give me hug."

The First Time I Died

Chapter 33

Time moved on and now it was 2003. As predicted by the doctors back in 1979, the injury to my neck from the car accident I was involved in became progressively worse. I had been living in pain on a daily basis for over twenty-three years. Now the constant pain was so severe that nothing I could do would make it go away. I felt like the tin man on the Wizard of Oz who had been left out in the rain and was rusting all over. My hands felt as though someone was constantly smashing them with a sledge hammer. My left arm felt like it was dislocated at the shoulder. I could no longer raise my left arm, hold things or make a fist. I had constant pain in the back of my head, neck and shoulders. The bottoms of my feet felt like someone was shredding them with a razor blade. My breathing was labored. If the haunting, routine nightmares from my PTSD in the service weren't enough to deprive me of sleep, the constant pain would. I could only sleep for brief intervals sitting up in a chair over a 24 hour period. I finally knew I had enough.

I could not continue living much longer like this so I sought medical help. I knew it would probably require surgery. I was also told by God that I had a rough road ahead of me. I was not sure if I was going to pull through what lay ahead. I tried to tell Ag what God had reveled to me but she did not want to hear it. The MRI X-rays with contrast had confirmed that I had developed bone spurs and cartledge growth on the interior of the disks in my neck during the twenty-three plus years since the injury. The spurs had penetrated my spinal cord and the growth had severely compressed the nerves in my spinal cord. After considering several opinions, the only conclusion was corrective surgery.

It was March 2, 2004 when I was scheduled for surgery of my cervical spine at Massachusetts General Hospital. It was explained to me by my doctor that with the advancement in medicine this procedure was approximately 90 percent successful. It was discovered during surgery that my neck was in worse shape than was originally thought. There was some permanent damage done to the nerves. My doctor entered from the front of my neck stating it made things less complicated. He had to completely remove four of the vertebrae in my neck. The wedges cut out of the disks were fairly good sized, which enabled the disks to be taken out from around the spinal cord. My doctor explained to me that he had to grind down the interior of the disks with dentist tools to remove the cartilage and bone spur material that had grown over the years. He also had to pick out quite a number of bone spurs that were logged in my spinal cord. He then decompressed the nerves in my spinal column. When he finished this he placed the disks back in my neck and took out a fairly large section of my hip bone to cover and then fuse the disks in place. Finally, he covered the entire area with a titanium plate that he screwed into the disks to permanently hold it in place. I was told by my doctor that the operation took about 8 hours to complete. I remember when I finally came around from the operation that I immediately noticed the pain in my arm, shoulder, hands and feet was gone in some areas and noticeably less in other areas. I could at least function now and was in a lot less pain. After a two day stay in the hospital I was sent home.

Two days after they had sent me home I had developed a fever of 104, the interior of my neck was very sore and swollen and the incision around my hip had developed a rash. I was having great difficulty speaking and I could feel the airway in my neck closing fast due to interior swelling. My wife called the hospital and they said to rush me back in. By the time I reached the hospital I could hardly talk or breath and the rash had spread like wildfire and was now covering my torso and upper legs. I remember being admitted and looking at this really young kid dressed in a doctor's uniform. Still trying to keep my sick sense of wise guy humor, I asked him if his mother knew that he had skipped school and was in here playing doctor. He didn't find that amusing and turned his back towards me. I then attempted to tell him that I couldn't breathe. He wasn't looking at me and he couldn't hear or understand me. The next thing I knew was I was floating over my body and this doctor hadn't realized I had stopped breathing. I was now looking down on my body and this doctor. After some time elapsed he finally turned around and realized that I wasn't conscious. Then, from my position near the ceiling of the room I saw a frantic team of doctors trying quite a number of attempted procedures in an effort to get me breathing again.

Everything then faded and I found myself covered in darkness in what I firmly believe was the valley of the shadow of death. It is a very scary, cold, pitch black place. I or my essence still existed. I was being looked down upon and examined by a very real presence. I kept my eyes downcast as I dared not look up at the presence, nor did I dare say anything. I felt this being's penetrating eyes staring at me. I felt very alone, very afraid and totally exposed. I don't know who the being was that was looking down on me; maybe it was the Grim Reaper people talk about, or maybe it was God. I knew that at this time my fate was being determined. It is the most humbling feeling anyone might experience. Looking back on it I guess I was suspended in that place until my fate was determined on whether I would live or die.

While my essence was being held in this place, I later learned that the doctors were frantically trying everything in their power to get me breathing. They tried sticking tubes down my nose, in my mouth, and quite a number of attempts were made to cut an airway in my neck. They were having difficulty as they could not penetrate the titanium plate and scar tissue. I was severely bleeding though my nose and mouth. The doctors later told that I had officially stopped breathing for over 3 minutes; in fact one of the doctors admitted to me it was closer to 7 minutes. Per the doctors my pressure was almost none existent, but the doctors stated that my heart had not stopped completely; I was basically brain dead. I was in a coma-like state. In fact, they were not sure even if I survived how much brain damage I would have. According to my wife I lost my mind years ago, so I guess there wasn't much I could have lost. All I know is first I was out of my body watching them from above, and then went and had my visit in the valley. Due to what I went through at this hospital I don't believe I was told the complete story by the doctors, as the doctors and the hospital were possibly negligent.

The surgeon's report stated that they finally were able to drill a hole in my throat and put in trachea tube. I was in the intensive care unit for three days. I know at that time I was passing in and out. The doctors didn't think I was going to make it and my pastor came in with the "oils." I was told later that patients in the beds on either side of me in the intensive care unit did not make it. I had developed "Strep A," commonly known as the flesh eating disease, starting at the hip site and now covering most of my torso, groin and upper portions of my legs. I also developed pneumonia, thrush, and I had a seizure. A part of my Thyroid was also removed. The doctors were all amazed that I was alive.

Four hours later with heads drooping they came out to my wife stating they just had gotten me stable and still had not as yet addressed the hip site and the "Strep A" infection. My wife can be quite forceful when she is upset. She was not very happy with the doctors and growled her command for them to get back in there and fix her husband! They had to reopen the hip site, cut and clean out all the dead tissue, put a wick in to drain the infection, and bombard the entire infected area with antibodies. I thank God that this disease did not get as far as destroying my muscles before the doctors were able to get it under control. The doctors told Ag that they had bombarded me intravenously with seven different antibiotics.

At one point I remember being slapped and screamed at, not in a gentle manner, in an effort to bring me back to life. When I finally came to I was unable to speak. I was alive but was not out of the woods. I was not able to have anything by mouth, including ice or water. I was not receiving any nourishment and after a little over a week the doctors told me they would have to put in a double PIC line. One line was to feed me and the other was to give me the antibiotics intravenously, as my veins were collapsing due to the strong antibiotics I needed to kill the disease.

The reason for the potent antibiotic was that it had to get into my bone to continue doing its work. The doctors had to be sure they killed all of the disease so there would be no chance it could return. The PIC line was an internally inserted catheter about 42 to 46 inches long. It was placed in my arm and snaked though a major artery or vein to my heart. There was a very large thick needle that was attached to this long catheter. I had to be awake during the insertion of this. They did not numb the area where this was inserted. I had to be able to tell the doctor when they were stuck in muscle or bone. Believe me; it was even more painful than it sounds. They eventually gave me pain medicine after the PIC lines were inserted.

The Second Time I Died

Chapter 34

I was in the hospital for three weeks now. While there I felt totally depressed and angry. "Why me? I thought I felt betrayed by who I thought was my most beloved friend, God. I didn't understand it. Had I done something that really had Him angry with me? I know the book, I know His words, and I know His promises. I still had no answers. I was starting to lose hope and starting to become bitter. How many times did my faith need to be tested?

It was around this time that I was told that the swelling in my neck should have gone down enough that the doctors could place a smaller trachea in my throat that would eventually allow me to speak and eat. The doctor explained the procedure. It did not sound like it was going to be fun. I was not too thrilled at the prospect of any more pain, but I knew this had to be done before they would let me leave the hospital. I had to be awake for this procedure too. It involved deflating the balloon that was placed down my throat that held the trach in place. The balloon also helped in keeping the swollen area open enough to let air through. Anything could happen when they deflated this balloon.

My wife was with me this time, holding my hand. They deflated the balloon in my trachea and at the same time quickly tried to shove this long tube down my throat, but my throat closed up immediately. My wife states when they deflated the balloon she saw my entire body drain and turn pale as my body collapsed in her arms. I on the other hand had experienced something much different!

At first I remember not being able to breathe along with excruciating pain. Then I felt myself being lifted out of my body again. This time as I floated upward, I floated up past the ceiling to a level plane. When I floated past the plane all of my pain disappeared in an instant and at the same instant my whole being was filled with the most wonderful feeling that I can't even begin to put into words. I can't begin to describe how wonderful it felt. I was of the Woodstock generation, and contrary to Mr. Clinton, I have to admit that I did inhale. In fact, if Mr. Jimmy Hendrix were to ask me, "Are you experienced?" I would have to answer, "Yes, I am very experienced." I was no angel. I have tried many drugs. I have had kidney stones before which produces serious pain and was given three consecutive injections of morphine to try to kill the pain. Pain medication or any medication only deadens the pain experience, but you still feel dull pain. This time it was different; all of my pain was completely gone! This experience was far greater than anything I could ever have even imagined. It is frustrating because it is so difficult to explain.

While still experiencing this joy, I floated to a place where there were a multitude of people. The people were so white they appeared transparent, somewhat like jellyfish are. They were all individually outlined in what appeared to be a brilliant gold light that somewhat resembled gold lit garland. They were all facing a bright golden yellow light off in the distance. All of the people had their backs toward me. I did not recognize anyone as I could not see their faces. I also could not see the source of the light they were all looking toward. I did not see Jesus, but felt a wonderful presence and I firmly suspect was He standing beside me. I did not go through or see any tunnel with white lights going past me as I traveled as reported by some people who have had out of body experiences. I know what I did see, and what I am reporting here, it was not a hallucination illusion or dream.

I do not think this was heaven. I do believe it was paradise. I believe all of the people were facing and looking out at heaven. I also believe that heaven was where the golden light was radiating from. I do not believe that paradise and heaven are the same place. When Jesus died on the cross, He said to the man being crucified beside him, "Today you will be with me in Paradise" (Note: Luke 23:43 NIV). I believe Jesus meant exactly what He said. I do not believe Jesus meant heaven. Again I state, "I do believe Jesus meant what he said and said what he meant." I think what Jesus referred to is an area outside of heaven. Heaven is the "main function hall," the place where the wedding feast takes place. A place that those chosen will be invited to enter after the final judgment takes place. I would compare it to what you would find at an elaborate wedding. The guests wait in a very nice reception area, exchanging pleasantries, until such time as they are escorted into the main function room. This reception area is like what paradise is and the main function room is heaven.

My experience seemed to last for only a brief period. I was allowed only a peek or glimpse. I was ecstatic, filled with unspeakable joy! Joy beyond comprehension, way beyond any high I have ever experienced. I can only describe it as "totally" awesome! I begged the Presence to let me stay but was told it was not my time as I felt myself being pulled down back into my body. I was furious as I came back into my body! As soon as I was drawn back through the plane all the pain returned! I remember hearing my wife screaming at me as I was coming around. My wife was screaming, "Don't you die on me! If you die I'll bring you back and kill you myself! You don't die on me!" The nurse was also screaming at me, but she seemed to be more upset about the extra paper work she would have to do if I passed on. I wanted them all to leave me alone and please let me die! Now I was really in a dilemma. I asked myself why He couldn't he just let me die? I wanted to stay there so badly. Why did He let me see that? Why wasn't I allowed to stay? Why did I have to come back? Why do I have to get so much pain? I believe and trust Him, why is He allowing this? The only answer was, "You're not done yet."

I have always had a hard time understanding why God permits so much pain. He didn't even spare his own Son's immense pain! To see the "mild version" of what Jesus went through I strongly recommend that you go and see the movie by Mel Gibson, "The Passion." Jesus suffered so much pain! God states in His written inspired word, the Bible, that He will never leave us or forsake us. He states He will not give us more than we can handle. He also says that all things work for good. Well I was sure having a problem with all this. If His word is not true, then he is no God! I admit it; I was angry with God and I wanted answers!

I am constantly being shown that God "is" true to his word and he has continued to show me "He is" the great "I am." I just never understood. I still don't profess to know it all or to completely know or understand God. No human can. God is immeasurably superior to any human in every way. Our puny minds are incapable of even coming close to completely understanding God. He allows us to understand only in part. I know now that I was blind and I did not know that I was blind. I heard about him before I had my back yard experience; but I had listened with deaf ears. I had only wondered if there "might" be a God before my experience. Even though I was angry, God doesn't change. God has really big shoulders. God can handle my anger; he knows me better than I know myself and he gives me the room I need to sort things out. He answered me, as always, with the still quiet, calm voice within my mind. I have learned to distinguish his voice from my own thoughts. First I heard, "Why not you? Are you, or are you not my servant?" Then I heard, "Do you still trust me?" I did not want to respond. I was still angry. Then in my mind's eye I was given a vision.

It wasn't the first time he has given me visions, and all but three of the visions have come to pass. I can't get into them all or I will never finish this book. I knew they were visions only after weeks for some, months and years for others. They came true exactly as they were shown to me in the vision. I am not able to see into the future, I am not a psychic and there is no other explanation for the accuracy of the visions of what happened in the future.

Getting back the vision I was given while in the hospital, first I was shown what appeared to be clear jello, then the jello turned into a single raindrop as it fell into the ocean. Then I saw all the oceans. I was then shown what appeared as a sand-colored wall. The wall turned into a single grain of sand. Then I was shown the sand on many beaches. I understood what God was showing me. My life here on earth was represented by the single raindrop and single grain of sand.

Even if I lived to be 150 it was nothing in comparison to eternity. I was then shown Christians being eaten by lions, Christians being staked alive, doused with oil and set on fire to light the streets of ancient Rome. Missionary's being tortured, raped and murdered all over the world. Then he reminded me of what the Apostle Paul said. Simply put, Paul said, "Think of all the sufferings you endure here and now as nothing in comparison to the riches and glory you will receive that will last for an eternity." The Apostle Paul was also familiar with pain. Paul had personal meeting with Jesus somewhat similar to that which happened to me. Paul was on the road to Damascus on his way to persecute the Christians when he had his experience. Paul was Saul the Pharisee, the prosecutor of the followers of Jesus. Paul was given much and he also suffered much for what he was given. Paul was taken out and beaten, stoned, whipped, flogged and jailed. Paul was shipwrecked; he spent a day and a night in the frigid ocean. When he made it to shore he went to warm himself over a warm fire and he was bitten by a viper. Paul should have died from the viper bite. The vision I saw in my mind's eye was quite clear and hit me right in the heart. The Apostle Paul just shook off the viper! He didn't die! God decided Paul wasn't done! God had more for Paul to do. "For those that much has been given, much will be required," are the words of Jesus.

It's not about me. It's not about you. The world does not

revolve because of us. It's all about God. As for me, the message was clear enough. I pondered the words of Jesus and I understand him, I know him. I may not know or understand him completely, but I do know him. Shake this off like Paul shook off the viper and go be a witness for God. All of the "chosen" true Christians "know" God and no matter what was or is done to them, including torture and a hideous death, they continued to choose to keep on trusting and holding on to their faith in Him. We must persevere until the end and not lose our faith no matter what happens to us. I understand where my brothers and sisters are coming from and so I do trust him, no matter what life has in store for me. God means what he says and says what he means. I felt his awesome presence and heard him clearly in my back yard that day; it was not a hallucination, dream, or illusion. It was not a windy day. No sane person would attempt to paint anything outside on a windy day as the wind would likely blow debris onto whatever was being painted and ruin the paint job. I know what I experienced and I will cling to Him.

It's All About Relationships

Chapter 35

God has opened my eyes to look at things from a different perspective. I took a good look at everything that has always been around me. God is all around us. As I stated earlier God holds everything together and allows everything to function. I had never noticed before. I took so much for granted. Now I could see so much and ask in wonder. Why doesn't the sun burn itself out? How is it that this planet rotates exactly, in the same rotation, it doesn't slow down or speed up? How is it that this planet is tilted at just the right angle and at just the right distance from the sun? Do you realize if we were any closer to the sun we would all burn up, any further away we would be frozen? Look at the human body, the human brain, ears, and eyes! We have just begun to understand how they all work. How does your heart know how to beat on its own, and your lungs, how do they know how to function even while we sleep? This was all designed way past human genius and in no way could have ever happened by accident. You would have a better shot of winning every lottery, every day for a million years and then some. Before my experience I thought if there was a God, I would not expect this superior being to get personally involved with puny humans. Before this experience I would question, if God does exist why doesn't he show himself to us? Why the mystery? Now I know; he did and he does, we just aren't paying attention.

When I met God that day in my back yard back in 1975 He knew that I would not be content until I found Him again. He planted the seed in me. I never formally studied theology in college. I am not an ordained minister. I'm just an ordinary lay person and so were the Apostles Peter, Matthew, James and John. They were ordinary men, fishermen and tax collectors. They all came to know God. I, as they, am just a servant, a messenger delivering my testimony along with a message. Even though I have had no formal training studying theology in college, I have done quite a bit of studying on my own. By the world's standard I guess I am not a total idiot. I hold a bachelor's degree from the last graduating class of Boston State College. My major was Business Management and my minor was in Psychology. I continued on with College Studies in Mathematics and Science and received my Massachusetts Department of Education Teaching Certification. I am a Massachusetts Department of Education certified teacher for Math, Earth Sciences, Business, and special subjects.

Again I strongly reiterate God says what He means and He means what He says. God put on a human body to come down here to dwell among us. In comparison to God we are less than babies. I will try to explain or illustrate how much God understands and loves us by using the comparison of my love and understanding of my grandson Jake. When Jake was born he was instantly loved by me. He could not, or did not, do anything to deserve this love. No matter what he does he is still loved completely, even when he does things that displease me. Even when he does wrong, he is and will always be my grandson. He is now eighteen months old. His vocabulary is very limited and he runs around the house like a mad man. I understand Jake and the world around him better than he does. I know what he likes and does not like. I know what mischief he would get into if left alone. Every detail of this child brings me abundant joy. I could watch him for hours. I can also appreciate his limited understanding and int_ of the world around him.

Jake loves these new Baby Einstein videos. He will r_ around, color where he is not supposed to, watch the videos and shovel a handful of cheerios in his mouth. I get down on the floor and bring myself down to his level to develop our relationship even further. I will stay beside him on the floor just basking in the joy of watching this little creature. He will watch the video for a few seconds, and then quickly look up to be sure I am still there with him. He talks to me in his language. He always has a smile on his face and looks at me while speaking the words "hi papa." I melt. He may not yet have the full capacity to understand me, but it doesn't matter as he knows he is loved. When he comes over to me my arms are always outstretched, his eyes are lit up and there is a smile on his face as he calls for me to hold him. It is a bond of love. I am in this child and he is in me, though we are two separate beings. He is my flesh and blood and I am his. Jake is an extension of me. This is also true with all my children. This is true with God the father, God the Son and God the Holy Ghost and God's interaction with us. Not only did God come down to our level because He loves us so much; He also allowed himself to be brutally humiliated, tortured and put to death for us in showing how much we mean to him.

In reading the New Testament you will find that not only did Jesus die for us, he also came back to life again. This fact was witnessed by thousands, not simply by just one man's account. No other religion can make this claim of its founder. As previously stated, in all of the other religious beliefs the founder still remains very dead. Jesus, on the other hand, is very much alive! As hard as it is to try and comprehend with our limited minds. This is the merciful, compassionate being that I met in my back yard. His name is Jesus and He is truly God.

It has never been about religion. It has always been and always will be all about a relationship! God is very much alive and God really does want a personal relationship with each relationship even closer than the one I have with [my] or children. God will not force this relationship [on us]. Love cannot be forced and be accepted. It is our [choice]. [Jesus] died for all of us who make the choice to accept this relationship. When we accept this fact we become God's children. Not all people can accept this and not all people are God's children.

The Bible states that God is all knowing. I would expect that only of God. The Bible states that in the beginning only God existed. The Bible proclaims in John:1 (NIrV) in the beginning, God (the Word) was already there. John continues stating the Word (God the Son) was with God, and the Word (God the Holy Spirit) was God. He (Jesus) was with God in the beginning. All things were made through Him (Jesus). Nothing that has been made was made without Him (Jesus). Life (God the Holy Spirit) was in Him (Jesus) and that life was the light for all people. John knew God; John knew Jesus. John ate with, walked with, and personally witnessed the miracles Jesus did. John personally talked and walked with Jesus (God). John wrote what he witnessed in the Bible.

God is the source who made everything. God is everywhere, in everything and holds everything together. Please note that this is what "energy" is and does. Energy is a life force. Without energy there is no life. We find that energy in everything, even in the air. Energy holds all matter together. Have you seen a hurricane, a tornado, an earthquake? There is no "mother nature"; it is God's creation. They are only minor manifestations of his mighty power. So if God is the source, then he is also, but not only, energy. Sounds heavy, doesn't it? Think about it a bit and you will get it.

We learn from science as a fact that energy cannot be created or destroyed. Energy can only be changed or be transformed from one form to another. For an easy explanation about energy transference, just find out where you get your electric power from and how it's produced. Some examples of how energy is transformed would be by water power, wind power, heat power, sun power and so on.

We as humans can plant a seed, fertilize it, water it, expose it to sunshine, but we can not bring a seed to life. The same applies to human or animal seeds; only God can give life. Doctors can give us medicine, perform surgery, but they cannot actually heal us. We can try to put the energy in things to bring them to life. With humans this only works with mechanical things. In the movie Frankenstein, it is energy transference from a lightning storm that supposedly brings the monster to life. It is interesting in this movie that man takes a dead body and tries to put the energy back into the dead body to bring it back to life. But that cannot be done by any man and it is only a movie made from man's imagination. Since God is the true energy source and God is energy, only God can put part of himself into bringing all the things that live and breathe to life and he is the energy source that holds all things together.

Science also proves that everything is made of "atoms." Atoms are part of energy. The Bible states in the Old Testament in the book of Genesis that God made the first humans. This is where the entire human race stems from, not apes. He called his creation man and named him Adam. It is interesting that it sounds like atom. Atoms are what everything is made from. God could have called Adam by some other name, like Bill, or Sue, but he didn't, he called him Adam. God states in the Bible that Adam was made from dust and that God first formed the dust then God blew life (energy) into the dust and produced man. God did not go into great detail; He just gave us the basics.

Stop for a second and use your own "reasoning ability." Adam was formed from dust and charged with energy. Our bodies that sustain us as our entity dwells within them are comprised of dust. It's the energy between every cell that holds them it together. Have you ever really looked at a corpse up close? It sounds a little morbid, but from a scientific point of view it is quite interesting. When we die what happens is that our bodies can no longer function properly in our environment. Our entity, energy, soul, spirit or whatever you want to label, it leaves the body. The remaining dead body lacks the energy that makes the person alive. The body then disintegrates back into dust. We can drain a corpse of blood and fluids. We can also put preservatives back into a dead body in an attempt to slow down the decaying process. In the end it still turns into dust that lacks the energy that holds it together and allows the body to function. We can even speed up the decaying process with cremation. Many people hold dear the remains of a loved one contained in jar that may sit on a mantle. Inside the jars we only find dust. This is all fact not a theory or a myth. So if the energy, entity or soul that was the person in the body is released from the body and this energy cannot be destroyed, where does it go? The energy or entity is not destroyed. It just lacks a body to function in.

Please think about this: how long is your life on this place called earth? Will you make it to 100? What will it profit you if you gained the whole world in that time frame? You can't take it with you when you go. Then I ask you to ponder this: when you do die, as all of us die, how long will you be dead? I strongly urge you to just check out the word "eternity," and as just a reminder, when your body dies, your "entity" or "soul" does not. Whether you want to take a hard look at this fact or not, your life here is just a tiny fraction of time in comparison to eternity.

Reason and Choice

Chapter 36

The Bible states that Adam and Eve were placed in what you could say was "Paradise Island." Adam and Eve didn't know it, but they had it made. There wasn't a thing they would need to worry about. All their needs were met. But they did not yet have "choice" or "reason," so they did not know that they had it made. Everything was taken care of for them, but they could not understand this as they did not yet have choice and reason. God is all-knowing, but they certainly were not. God knew that evil "had to" eventually enter the picture; if not, Adam and Eve would be no more than puppets. God knew, even though He forbid Adam and Eve to eat the fruit from the tree of knowledge, they would do what God told them not to do. God knew what they would do before they did it. God knows us all. Adam and Eve had the ability to simply trust God to take care of them. But that was not enough, for they did not totally trust God, so they had to be shown and they had to learn this trust as we all do. Without this trust we are doomed.

Without evil there could be no choice. Think about it; how would you know what compassion was, without knowing what suffering is? How could it be explained? How would you know if something is good unless you know what is bad? Think of all the things that you would never know, like grace, mercy, tenderness, love!

Choice and reason are essential. Without them we could

not have free will. Not many people really think about this. Webster Dictionary defines choice as "to select." Webster Dictionary defines reason: "To think; the power of comprehending, inferring, or thinking in orderly rational ways, proper exercise of the mind, the sum of intellectual powers, to take part in conversation, discussion, or argument, to talk with another as to influence his actions or opinions." I think my most favorite passage in the Bible is Isaiah 1:18. "Come let us reason together, saith the Lord, though your sins be as scarlet, I will make them white as snow!" This is a very personal invitation concerning a personal "relationship" with God. God is stating that He is willing put any offense aside and talk things out with us reasonably. To be able to reason you need to have choice. We are given "free will." Free will is our choice to accept things or reject them.

When Adam and Eve ate the fruit from the tree of knowledge, their minds were opened. This is where "choice and reason," the knowing good from bad, began. Then we see in Genesis 3:22 something amazing; then the Lord said, "Now that the man has become like us, knowing good from bad." Can you grab this! First of all the "like us." God is stating "us," as in more than single person here. In referring to the "us" God had to be addressing equals. This is the first acknowledgement of "another" or "more than one" God. God was speaking to God the Son and God the Holy Spirit.

Now Adam and Eve are no longer puppets, but creatures that can think, reason, and understand. This also allows for a higher level of relationship. This happened as the direct result of the introduction of evil. It now became possible for humans to think, reason and understand in communication. Now we can know what kindness, compassion, mercy, grace, sorrow, pain, suffering, joy, hope and love are all about; and the list goes on my friends. Your life while you are alive here on earth is school! Your brief, and I do mean brief, especially when you compare it to eternity, time here on earth will determine where your entity gets to go for an eternity. We are given the ability to "reason" and even given a "choice"! The hard fact is that we can now see how bad evil can be. God allows evil as we have to "know" how bad evil really is to ever "know" how good, good is. God does not take pleasure in suffering. No parent enjoys watching their child suffer.

When we learn, we also learn what we can and cannot trust in. This is where faith enters the picture. Faith is a verb. A verb means action. When my children were small they stepped out in faith and trusted that Daddy was going to make sure they were safe would not let them drown when they jumped into the swimming pool. They needed to take those first steps and jump into the pool. Those first steps were faith in action. We have both a reason and a choice to either believe that God exists or not. We have the choice to put our faith in God. Our faith requires our action. We need the faith to seek God and to we need to choose to trust in God. If we are sincere and want to find God, we can! He allows it for anyone who is seeking him for the right motives. In seeking to find God, keep in mind to pay Him the respect and honor He so rightly deserves. We cannot even fathom His intelligence. He knows each and everyone of us. He knows all our thoughts and true motives. He knows what actions we will take and under what conditions before we do. God cannot be fooled. He is not out to get us! He made us and He knows that we are only talking, walking dust. God doesn't need anything from us. God made everything from nothing and everything already belongs to God.

God has every right to make all the rules; we don't. Remember, we are just dust, just clay in the hands of the potter. God made and loaned us bodies or vessels to house our entities. These bodies allow us to function within them while we are here on earth.

The Sacrifice

Chapter 37

God also placed himself into the body of a man and walked the earth he created. Again, His name is Jesus. I state the word "is" because He "is" alive. Most people did not, and some still do not recognize Him as God. Jesus, the Messiah, the anointed One, God the Son, who took off his royal deity and allowed His entity to be encased in a human body. Jesus did this for a few reasons, one of which was so that we humans could see what God is like and what God expects from us His creation. The other reason was because we humans needed to be saved from destroying ourselves. God knows that we can't save ourselves, let alone save anyone else. So if anyone of us is to be saved, God has to do the saving. God would have to provide the sacrifice since He alone is pure and perfect. That's where Jesus comes in; Jesus allowed himself to be "the needed human sacrifice." Jesus is God, so then only Jesus can do the saving. I stated earlier in this book that "a" human "sacrifice" was needed as payment for our breaking Gods rules, or put into other words; committing sin. In further explaining what was stated earlier in this book, God requires the shedding of blood for payment of sin. The sacrifice had to be a pure animal with no blemishes in the Old Testament times. An unblemished lamb or goat was generally used. If the family was poor a dove could be sacrificed. But an animal is not a human. The animal sacrifice was only used as a temporary solution. One unblemished or pure and perfect human was needed. The final and full sin offering would need to be done by an unblemished, sinless person. Since no human is unblemished or sinless, God had to provide the sacrificial lamb, as He did for Abraham. Jesus is the full and final sin offering, the innocent unblemished lamb that was sacrificed.

Jesus was tortured and nailed to a cross as a criminal, although he did nothing wrong. He placed His entity in a human body and allowed Himself to be tortured and crucified. He could have avoided it all by simply saying he was not God. No sane or insane person would cling to their story under such torture unless it was all true. The Roman soldiers severely beat him and whipped him with leather that was embedded with lead. They actually whipped his skin off, exposing His bones. They made a crown of thorns and shoved it down into his head. Then they drove spikes though his hands and feet, nailing him to a cross. The spikes were driven into him at the base of the hand at the wrist to support his weight. When a person is crucified they eventually suffocate to death, as the person's own body fluids fill the lungs, cutting off the oxygen supply in the lungs. It is a slow and very painful death. No one sane or insane would allow all that continue knowing that it could easily have been stopped. All of this is in the Bible and it is also verified in historical records. As I stated, all Jesus had to do was to say that He lied, He wasn't God. That's all He had to do, but He wouldn't do it. He couldn't say it, because He told the truth; He is God, God the Son. If Jesus did not die there would be no shedding of innocent blood and no atonement of sin for us.

Jesus wouldn't even allow himself the simple taste of the gaul, a numbing agent, which was offered to him as he hung on the cross. Jesus knew he needed to endure the full pain for the payment of our sins. God made the rules; all that is required of us is to believe it and put our faith and trust in God. It's as though we were little children drowning and God has come to our rescue. We have to understand this as fact. God the Son was not murdered for nothing. Rejecting this fact is the highest insult to God. It's like spitting in His face and throwing His gift back at his feet. What do you think God will do to those who reject this gift? He is willing to forgive us to the point of dying for us. What could anyone ever do that was worse than what God went though for us that God would not forgive us for?

Jesus has accepted us "as is" and has paid the ultimate price in our place. Jesus saved us and continues the work He started in us. Please let me stress this: "Jesus" is the only one that can do the "saving"! This is why He is known as the Savior of all of us that choose to come to Him to be saved.

Though Jesus died on the cross, He also arose from death. This fact was witnessed by many. He promises that all who repent of their sin, believe that He "is," not "was" (as He still lives, and I speak from first hand experience) God, believe that He forgives you of your sin, believe that He died on that cross in payment for your sins and then He rose from the dead will be saved. All we need to do is not doubt this fact, fully trust him, fully put our faith in him and He will save us. Remember what I explained about Adam and Eve and why this is so sensitive to God. All that "choose not" to believe this will not get to live with God when they pass on from their life in this world. When their body expires, their entity is doomed.

Developing the Relationship

Chapter 38

As I stated, God accepts us as we are with all our dirty baggage. Over time God turns our lives around as He teaches us what He expects of us as He dwells within us. We need to learn this if we are to come and live with Him for an eternity. We have to trust him with our whole being and do the best we can to live the way He wants us to. He will make up the difference. He will show you as He has shown me. Trust in this truth, He will change and mold you, "over time," if you choose to let Him. He does not force Himself on anyone. Jesus stated that He is the vine and we are to be the branches. The branch cannot live without be attached to the vine. Only the vine can give life to the branch. Only the vine can produce the fruit that sprouts from the branch. What is needed to produce the fruit comes from the vine, not from the branch. This is how God works in those that choose to have this relationship with Him.

We can only enter into a relationship with God when we truly seek him with a pure heart. You will find God only when you seek God the Son: Jesus. Before you seek out God, you need to examine yourself. You have to be totally honest with yourself. You have to know His rules then you have to examine your own shortcomings in following His rules. You have to confess your shortcomings to God in seeking His help in your life. You need to ask for His forgiveness for offending Him by breaking his rules. You have to be willing to let Him take over the control of your life and allow Him to mold you. Only God can save you, from even you! Listen, no matter how bad you think you are, if you know what you did was wrong and in total honesty and confess it as wrong, God will forgive you.

In a caring, loving relationship, whether it is with a spouse, a parent, a child, or a best friend, you know the other person. If you do something that offends this other person, it affects the relationship you have with them. Feelings are hurt and communication breaks down. If you really care or love the other person in the relationship the situation will bother you and haunt you until it is made right. Sometimes it will be made right with a sincere apology and the promise not to repeat whatever it was that was offensive. When your apology is accepted, the relationship continues.

But suppose in time, you go and do the same thing again, only to find yourself in the same old mess? Will you be forgiven? Sometimes we humans have hard hearts and we do not forgive. God is beyond us and God, will forgive for He is also love. True love is unconditional. To illustrate I can think of several examples. The battered wife or girlfriend who always takes back the one that abused them. Another example is one shared with me by my friend Billy. Billy passed away recently, but I will always remember his story. Billy was Bird's brother. Billy worked as a social worker for the state. Billy once told me about this 7 year old little girl.

The girl had no parents and was being raised by her paternal grandfather. Billy, accompanied by a constable and a female co-worker had to go into the inner city to take the little girl away from her grandfather. The little girl had severe gonorrhea that she had contracted from her grandfather. As the girl was taken away, although she had been constantly abused by her grandfather, she was screaming hysterically wanting to be taken back to him. No matter what the offense, unconditional love forgives.

If we really love God and we do what offends him it will

eat away at us until we have a change of heart and change our minds, coming to the conclusion that God is right. This change of heart and mind is what is known as repentance. If we have this change of mind and agree with God and confess our error and ask His forgiveness, He will forgive. If we don't do this, He will allow us to continue to stew in the consequences. Sometimes we will even ignore our conscience. If we do, things only get worse for us. God disciplines his children.

To have a personal relationship with God requires that the individual be born of the Holy Spirit. God seals you with God the Holy Sprit. This is referred to as being "born again" God the Holy Spirit will teach and help guide you through life. God the Holy Spirit will come and live "in" you. Again, this can only be done by God. You only need to trust God to do this; you can't feel it happening. Again, Jesus talks about being born again in the Gospels. When you become born again you don't automatically turn into some "Holy Roller." It doesn't work like that. There's no big "Poof!" and you automatically turn into this perfect being. Now God will dwell within you and then you will dwell in God. When this happens you become a new creature and a true child of God. Over time you will discover you have a new nature. You will know that this has happened to you mainly in hind sight. This has happened to thousands if not millions of people over the past 2000 or so years.

When God is with you He will help you with your struggles in life. You no longer will face anything alone. This may sound strange or hard to understand, but it's what happens and is not based on what you feel. All that I have explained that happens is not based on your feelings. If you do not feel this happening to you that is normal, it still happens. Again, through this personal relationship with God, over time He will change your heart and mind so that you find you are being transformed into someone that is more in line and equipped with a heart and mind that is similar to that of Jesus. Other people and their needs will be more important to you than your needs. Through this relationship you learn to trust God and put your life in his hands. You learn to trust Him even in the hardest of times or most difficult situations. You must have this child-like faith. You can't see what life has in store for you, only God can. You just have to trust Him, learn to lean on Him to get you through. Through this process of trusting you will learn what true faith is all about. True faith pleases God, without true faith you cannot please God.

Being born again, you are now one of the "chosen," a true Christian, an adopted child of God. You will see that something happened, something is different in time. A seed was planted within you. Your life will change from "what's in it for me" or a "me" centered life, to a life that puts God in the center over time. You will become a branch as Jesus will be the vine. The vine will make the branch grow and produce fruit. Being chosen or considered a true Christian is not based on our good deeds. It does not matter how you good you think you are. You cannot get into heaven by being good enough. If you are not as good as Jesus you fall far short of God's acceptable "good enough" standard. It is impossible for any human to follow all of God's rules and never mess up, even once. What is impossible for humans is possible only by God. God-produced good deeds, are what God is looking for. You will find more and more over time that you will naturally want to please God.

As you grow you will find that you will have a new nature. A nature that now puts others and their needs ahead of your own. Your sins will be forgiven, due only by reason of God's gracious pardon due to what Jesus did for you and me on the cross. But you won't have a free license to keep on sinning either, even though your future sins are also forgiven. You don't automatically become sinless. What you will find is that you will start to sin less, and less, and still less, over time.

God has His ways in dealing with His children and sin usually has consequences. God allows the consequences to happen to us in response to what we have done. It will help you to stop doing what isn't right. He also helps you in changing your mind on how you see things. Sin will become less attractive to you over time. You will find that you naturally won't want to do whatever sin it is that holds you as its captive. The sin you used to love to do will begin to lose its appeal. Then you will eventually stop doing it. You will have a complete change of mind about the "sinning" and no longer have the desire to do it.

Your thoughts about things will start changing over time. It will be like you got wiser somehow. You might even realize that what you had once thought were your thoughts are really God, the Holy Spirit, speaking to you, as you were never that smart. You may have thought some things were okay or acceptable before this change happened to you. Now you might have a different view and see that these things are not okay. Again, slowly, over time and in hind sight, you will notice how much you have changed and grown. You will also start to see, understand and agree with God why certain things are not good. You know there is a saying what comes around goes around. If you do certain things that are not right to others, don't be amazed when someone does the same things to you.

There Is a Reason

Chapter 39

I have met quite a number of people who argue out of pure ignorance. These people are positive they are right but have never bothered to check out the true facts. Before you defend a position, be sure you have checked out the facts. To really get to know God and develop this new relationship that you now have with God requires that you know God's word. God's word can easily be found in the Basic Instructions Before Leaving Earth handbook, commonly referred to as the Bible. The Bible is the Human Basic Operating manual. To understand some of the Bible you will need God's help. If you are in God and God is in you then God the Holy Spirit will guide you as you study the Bible. You just have to ask for God to help you. If you attempt to read the Bible without God's help, parts of the Bible may not make much sense to you. You also should seek out the help of other true Christians, or true believers, as a safety check that helps keep you on the right path. This is what is known as fellowship with other believers. The Bible may appear to some people as just another book, or a book full of myths, legends and inconsistencies. I assure you, it is not.

There are all kinds of laws that exist. You break government law, you get punished. Ignorance of the law is no excuse; you still get punished. There are laws of science. You ignore them, and you will get hurt. Take the law of gravity for instance. Try jumping off a tall building without a parachute;

you'll most likely be hurt or worse. Consider God's laws. If I commit adultery, someone is going to hurt. Even If I murdered someone, I might be very lucky and get away with it as far as the law is concerned. But you really don't get away with anything, because something inside of you changes you and eats away at you. God made everything, including you. You came in this world with no personal belongings and that's how you will leave this world. As I stated before, the only thing that you will take into eternity is your entity with its memories. Again, God sets the rules, not you, not me, and whether you chose to believe it or not, it's still the way it is.

Some people choose to not believe in God as they see so much wrong in the world, so much evil. So how could God exist and allow evil to continue. But you see, as I have stated, evil must exist for choice and reason to exist. If evil must exist, suffering and pain must also exist. But, who will bear it? God did, for one. So if He was willing to suffer severely unto death, am I so special that I can't be willing to bear suffering as well? Granted, I am not God, nor do I dare to presume I could have gone through what Jesus went through. I have tasted a bit of what Jesus suffered, just a bit. Someone has to experience suffering and pain, otherwise we all will never get to appreciate or understand what it is like; quite a number of feelings and emotions would never be allowed to be expressed. There would be no understanding of expressed grief, sorrow, sadness, compassion, mercy, grace and so much more. Keep in mind that you carry your memories within your entity when you leave this school called earth. We learn from our experiences and from the experience of others.

How many of us have ever had a sick child and begged God to spare the child from the suffering and pain they were in. We would be willing to bear the pain and suffering ourselves so our child could be spared. That's exactly what God did for us, His children. Sometimes pain and suffering makes us stronger or strengthens our immune system. I know there are times when a child is not spared and I know the grief associated with it. Believe what I am telling you. Although it is very hard to accept, there is a reason for every believe that a child taken by God has done a g God. The child has performed their task here on lives with God in pure happiness and everlasting

My younger sister, Lori, was taken from an early age. God had a job for her to do and although I miss her, I feel that she also did her job well. She suffered for many years until God decided her task was done here and he freed her from her broken shell, her broken body that she functioned through while here on earth. From her life, my family knows pain and suffering. As does anyone who knew my sister. We have to know how badly, bad can be, if we are ever to know how good, good can be. Someone has to carry the burdens; the task assigned them by God. My sister carried hers well. I remember the last time I saw her. I did not want to go in her hospital room, knowing it would probably be the last time I would see her alive. The pain I felt inside was too great. As she was lying in that hospital bed, she was crying. She told me that she was afraid and did not want to die. She was piercing my soul with a stake as I would look at her and hear her words.

I held her and whispered to her, "I know, I know. Do you believe what I told you about Jesus," I asked. She said she did. I told her she had to trust Him now more than ever. I asked her to promise me. She said yes. I did get to tell her I loved her and she said the same to me. She died shortly there after in my father's arms.

If you read the Bible you will come across the book of Isaiah of the Old Testament. Please note chapter 6 verses 8 though 10 in particular. I would also at the same time refer you to please note Romans chapter 8 verses 29 through 33 in the New Testament (for easy reading see the NIV). Now I would like to offer you the following. God states in the Bible that through God the Son all things were made. God the Son existed before He came down here to earth and allowed His entity to dwell within a human body. God also knew John the Baptist before he was placed into a human body. He knew all of his own children, his chosen, even before they were placed

...man bodies. Now imagine for the moment that before ... were placed into their human bodies, that they all existed ...ith God. Just suppose God came and asked of his chosen, "Some way suffering and pain in all of its various forms must be displayed so the people I have created can learn." God then asks, "So, who will go for Us? It won't be very long and I will be with you, so who will go for Us?" I believe my sister must have raised her hand and agreed to do the task assigned to her. I guess I must have raised my hand for the part I am playing. Then there were others that agreed to play the part of innocent children or people that are tortured, raped and murdered. Still others agreed to play the parts of grieving parents, friends or relatives of these victims. Do you see? Everyone has a part to play, everyone has a purpose. Life really is a split second in time when compared to eternity. From the first second we are born, each second that passes brings us closer to our final destination; our death. No one escapes. Learn while you still have time down here on earth.

Something Worse Than Hell

Chapter 40

Please remember this: God owes us nothing. God also has choices. There really is a devil and there really is a hell, even if you chose not to believe it. It still exists. Hell is a holding area, a place opposite that of paradise. It was prepared and intended for occupancy by Lucifer, known as Satan or the devil, and the rebelling angels who are known as demons. By the way, the devil isn't a red guy with horns and a tail. Lucifer was the head angel he had a superior intelligence, he was very powerful, he was quite attractive, very well adorned and when he spoke it sounded like a symphony. He is also referred to as the prince of this world, the prince of the power of the air, the father of all liars and an angel of light. He isn't stupid; he knows us and our weaknesses. He also knows how to tempt each of us. He is full of pride and we humans are no match for him. God created him and only God can deal and easily handle Lucifer the devil.

There is also someplace that is worse than hell. This place is called the lake of fire. I find many people confuse hell with the lake of fire. The lake of fire is described in the Bible as the place containing a fire that never goes out, the place of eternal torture, a place where you can experience all the pain, yet never die. The facts are that hell is thrown into this place along with death, the devil, the demons, and anything or anyone whose name is not found in the Book of Life. This place is also called the second death, the place opposite of heaven at the final judgment.

The final judgment is where those who made the right choice, those waiting in paradise, get to enter that great banquet hall called heaven. Those that didn't make the right choice, who are likely to be found in hell, eventually get to be thrown into the lake of fire.

But maybe you're counting on something like this: "I'm not so bad, why so and so is so much worse than me, why I can't believe that a compassionate God would ever send someone like me to a place like that." Okay, only for argument's sake, let's say it's your way, even though you're the clay and just supposing that God doesn't mean what he says. Since God also has a choice, what if he decided to just take "his" big ball called earth crush it and go home? If you couldn't follow his rules like he told you to down here, even when he made a way for you to do so, whatever makes you think he will invite you to come and stay at his place? Remember when your body dies, that's all that dies. You live on as an "entity."

Jesus does note that some are cast into the outer darkness where there is wailing and gnashing of teeth. Say for argument's sake that you don't get sent to hell or the lake of fire but instead you get stuck in the outer darkness. Now just imagine for a moment, here you are, an entity without a body, and there is nothing, just black nothing, that you get to spend an eternity with. You don't want God and his rules, you want your rules. You don't want to believe in God as you don't want anyone or anything controlling you. Now you are in the outer darkness without a body, so go ahead and have it your way, make something from nothing. You can't get to God's place, and then again you're not invited! You'll have plenty of time to ponder, sulk, cry, grit your teeth in anger if you could (but then you won't have any teeth anymore), or do whatever, while you float in nothing but outer blackness. In fact you will have an eternity. That is, unless of course you can make a body for yourself out of nothing! Please, consider this book a wake up call. You do have a choice while you still have time.

Live By What You Believe

Chapter 41

Mother Theresa and Billy Graham, most people know who they are. They are not, nor were they ever looking for any human praise. They don't look to be placed on pedestals or worshipped. They are not flashy, nor do they call attention to themselves with fancy dress. They are servants of God; they are his children. Look at how they have lived their lives. They are a witness to the fact that God dwells within them, "look at their fruit." They are branches and their fruit that shines in this world was produced by the vine. The vine is God who lives within them. They live lives that show God is the center of their lives. They were not worried about what was in it for them. I see their fruit and know how they chose to live. I know when they say they are Christians that they do know God and that they are speaking the truth. I witness that they "live by" the truth they believe. They are "examples" of what it means to be "chosen" a true adopted child of God. They are an example of how to live a life here on earth with Jesus at the helm. I am sure they are not perfect, but I can see their fruit and believe they walk with Jesus! They put God first in their lives.

Becoming a Christian does not mean that you can now stroll though life without any problems, headaches, suffering, or pain. These things are allowed to continue. Sometimes in professing to be a Christian things even get worse. I find this happens a lot with new Christians as their faith is tested; as soon as trouble enters their lives they're usually ready to abandon ship. The hard times are tests; they show us where we truly stand in our faith. What you will come to learn in time is that these things are just other obstacles that God will help us to overcome. You will see, not when you are going through the experiences, but in hind sight, that they strengthen you and make you the diamond you were always meant to be. If God can forgive and change a scoundrel like me, what's your excuse? If you find that life is dealing more than what you think you can handle, hang in there, don't stop trusting God and don't abandon the ship. Don't give up, don't lose your faith. Look at my life. Do you think I have had it easy? Believe me, my life has not been a picnic in the park. Over the next year I know I have to face another major surgery. I don't know what the outcome will be, but I do know I just have to keep my faith in God.

I have only given you the reader glimpses of my life; there were a lot more unpleasant experiences I chose not to share. I have been with the bluebloods of Boston and society's outcasts; the snobs and the street people. I've seen the best and the worst of people. No one is better than anyone else; we are all on the same level in Gods eyes. We all have to eat, we all have to void, we all are born and we all will die. God accepts all people, even the murderers. No one has any excuse; God has shown us enough to choose. Some people choose to see it and some chose not to see. But God has made a way for man to be reconciled to himself. Jesus did not die for nothing.

There are many people who claim to be Christians but their life proves them to be something else by the examples of how they live and the choices that they make. There will always be weeds growing with the grass. The wolves that hide disguised as sheep are in every organization. Don't give up your faith, and trust in God over bad deeds done by human beings. Again I say do not put people on pedestals, don't put your faith in any human. Put your faith in God alone. Always remember to err is human. God will sort it all out in the end. Try to be patient and wait for his good timing. There's a reason for everything and all we do matters. Everything and everyone has a purpose. It's far bigger picture than our puny minds can ever fathom.

Many great people "know God": Abram, Isaac, Jacob, Moses, George Washington, Abraham Lincoln, most all of the founding fathers of America and many, many others. These people were just people, they were not fools or idiots and they all "knew God." God worked and lived through all of them. Even though they have passed on from this world, they are alive with God. They still know God, as only their bodies died; they live on. God does not want to be your enemy, your destroyer. This is not His intent. He wants you to "know Him personally" and to develop a relationship that will last for an eternity. God won't ever force himself on anyone. There is a simple reason for this. Just think about it, how could you love someone that you are forced to love? Love can only be freely given and freely received.

As I stated, to get to really know God, you need to read the Bible, the real Bible, not the book of Mormon, the Koran, or the Watchtower. You might want to start by reading the New Testament, particularly the books Matthew, Mark, Luke and John. These guys were just men, ordinary people, not theology students, not Gods. Think of them as news reporters if you like. They wrote what they saw, heard and did. Read through the New Testament then read the Old Testament. Read the Bible from cover to cover. It is not a book of myths and legions. The entire book is correct; it is our lack of understanding that creates our problems. After finishing reading the Bible, read it again, and again, and again, slowly. Ponder as you read, meditate and study what you have read. Each time you read the Bible you will find something new. You will find something you missed or something you did not understand before. The words will start to come to life right before your eyes. You will see a miracle. Then you will understand and know why it is referred to as the living word of God. It's a mandatory book or owner's manual for living here on earth. It is also not contradictory, even if some parts seem like they are. Again, the problem lies in our mind's limited ability to understand. Some parts may be hard to believe, but as I stated, *every* word of the Bible is true. You will discover a hidden world you were never conscious of. Jesus is the key to the entire Bible, both Old and New Testaments. If you read the Bible *you will* get to know God.

Talking to God

Chapter 42

God also wants you to pray to him. Not like some believe what prayer is. We humans really screw this up. Prayer *isn't* saying repetitive words over and over again. How would you like it if you were on the other side of a conversation, hearing the same old thing over and over again? How boring would that be? I know if I had to listen to same old thing over and over again, I would run the other way just to get away from the person. That's not what God wants. To pray to God just means to talk to him; just you and him in a conversation, alone, like a child would talk to his or her respected parent or your respected friend or mentor. Talk to him as a parent or friend that you love, look up to and respect Him with your whole heart. His every word back to you will be like a gift of gold. He wants you to tell him anything and everything. He already knows everything. He wants to hear it from you. Remember he already knows you! He knows your thoughts and motives. He wants you to get to really know yourself as well. He wants you to be honest with yourself and talk to Him about you and Him. He wants you to share your true feelings.

Share even the smallest detail with Him. You don't always have to do this on your knees. Just talk to Him with the respect He so deserves. You can talk to him in your closet or your car while driving down the road. Just be sure to talk to Him as much as you can every day. Sometimes I even pray or talk to God asking for parking spaces, and more often than not He provides. He does not always give me what I ask him for though. This is easy to understand if you are a parent. God will not grant me a selfish request. I don't give my own kids everything they ask me for either. Sometimes I know they really can't handle what they ask me for. Sometimes I won't give them what they ask for because it's not safe or good for them. Sometimes I won't give them something that might be a waste of money. Then sometimes I don't give them what they ask for as it will wrongly affect someone or something else. Sometimes I just don't want to spoil them. Like so many other people, I have even asked God to let me win the lottery. I even promised to give 20% to the poor if God would only let me win. It is pure selfish motive. To date I have never hit the lottery and most likely never will. It would be purely self-serving if I did win and would most likely spoil me. It probably would make me prideful or pull me away from depending on God for my needs. You don't need to be a rocket scientist to understand this logic and it is easier to understand if you are a parent.

    I'll give you another small example of interacting prayer or talking with God and how he responded to me. I remember one time my wife and I were headed over to my in-laws for a Saturday afternoon birthday party. My wife had to pick up a card at the store in the town square. I waited in the car for her. It was fairly quiet and there wasn't much traffic. Then as I looked out my front windshield I noticed an elderly man stepping into the crosswalk. He had a cane and was having trouble moving quickly. The light had changed from red to green and this man was still about a third of the way into the crosswalk. Then I saw a car load of kids speeding down the road towards the town square and towards the man. They saw him but the light was green and they were not going to stop. They missed the man by a fraction of an inch. He went flying backwards and landed in the middle of the street. The kids were hanging out the window screaming obscenities at "the old man" shouting that he get "the whatever" out of their way. The whole thing happened right in front of me. I went to get out of my car to help the man, but a group of people were there ahead of me and had come to his aid. I sat there with excited rage directed toward those kids. I was all alone in my car. I looked up to the sky and shouted out to God. I said, "Come on, God! That's not right!" You saw that and I saw that! That just isn't right!" I told my wife what happened when she came out of the store and life went on.

We went to the party, went home that night and went to bed. It was a summer evening. All the windows in the house were open and you could hear an occasional car going by our house and the traffic out in the distance. We lived about a mile from the town square, close to an intersection of main roadway. I don't know why, but around two-thirty in the morning something woke me up. I tossed and turned trying to get back to sleep. About a half hour later as I was still awake I decided it was time I tried the milk and cookies. I got up and went into the kitchen.

From our kitchen bow window you could see the whole intersection and the church that was across the street. I was standing in the kitchen in my underwear eating the cookies and drinking the milk. I heard the scream of tires off in the distance racing through the town and heading towards my house. I also heard the police sirens not far behind the screaming car. As the car was getting closer a scary thought crossed my mind. I thought in considering the speed this car was going they would not be so foolish as to try to turn at the intersection and head up my street. They were going to fast and they would never make the turn. Low and behold, that's exactly what they did. They hit the telephone pole in front of the church head-on! You can just imagine what I felt! I was about to go running out in my underwear before realized that was all I had on.

I scrambled for a pair of pants and rushed out the door as I was putting them on. The car had hit the pole with such force that I thought the occupants would all be dead. As I was approaching the car the police had just pulled up. To my astonishment these were the same kids that almost ran over "the old man." The trunk of their car was wide open and full of beer.

The driver was pinned in behind the steering wheel. The front seat passenger went through the windshield and one kid had gotten out of the back and was attempting to make a run for it. The police caught him in short order and I must add that they were not very gentle with him. They were all alive, which was a miracle in itself. I just couldn't believe it. I saw it all right before my eyes and was totally amazed! I looked up at the sky and said "Okay, God!" He knew what I meant.

I'll talk to Him about when I'm worried, when I feel down, when I feel so much love for Him I think I will burst, when I think He painted an exceptional sunset, when He shows me something great and I know it was all Him, when I'm not happy with some of the things He has me go through and when I am angry with Him. Again, God has pretty big shoulders and an abundance of forgiveness when I come back to Him and apologize for the times I am being an idiot.

Child-like Faith

Chapter 43

God sees our whole lives from beginning to end. With God there is no time as we know it here on earth. He knows what actions or inactions will affect "whatever or whomever." Therefore God allows some things and does not allow other things. Try seeing God in the example of the parent, child relationship. For those of the readers who have children; do you always give in to your child's demands and let them have their way? Or in being a parent do you refuse to give in to the child's demands because you know it isn't the best thing for them? How many parents have brought their child to a doctor knowing he was going to give them a shot? How many parents have taken their child to a dentist? Does the child ever try to talk the parent into not taking them?

When children are very young they have a great deal of trust. They have child-like faith. This is the same faith that we need to please God. Think about bringing your child to the doctors for a immunization shot, or to the dentist. The child trusts you and you knew all along that you were bringing them to a place or person that would deliver them pain. But you, as the parent, knew it was in their best interest and it had to be done. Did your child give up on you and no longer trust you for what you put them through? How many of you have been told by your child almost as their last resort that they hate you! Or that they don't love you anymore! Only to have them hug and kiss you the next day and even tell you they are sorry for what they said? You don't think we act like that with God? Sure we do! We might even out of stubbornness refuse to pray to God or refuse to believe in Him. We blame God for everything because we don't understand, we can't understand, our intelligence is limited. How many parents out of love for their child would trade places with their child to spare the child from some pain, illness or even death? Again, remember that God did that for us.

There is quite a bit more information that God did not allow into the Bible. Just because something it is not talked about does not mean it never happened. There is quite a bit more that Jesus did that does not appear in the Bible as well. God allows us what information he feels is sufficient for us to make a choice. So, do so. God speaks in the Old Testament about those who will be "grafted" in, so to speak, to the Jewish nation, those who are to be "chosen as children of God." He states they will be given a new name and that name is "Christian."

Many people claim to be Christians. Many horrible things are also done by people claiming they do things in the name of Christianity. Many cults also claim they are Christian based. But I am telling you for a fact that being a true Christian, one chosen by God, an adopted child of God, one who will spend an eternity with God, all has more to do about the relationship with God than it does about any religion. Jesus plainly states that at the final judgment, many who claim they did all sorts of good things still won't be invited to dwell in heaven. Jesus sums it up for those people by stating, "I never knew you" (Matthew 7:23). Jesus was asked how you could identify a true Christian. He replied, "By their fruit" (Matthew 7:15). In another passage he stated that you can know if you are true Christian from your love of one another. In still another he states, "By their fruit," as I spoke of earlier.

My Soul Mate

Chapter 44

Although I did not know it when I first laid eyes on my Aggy; God had chosen her for my soul mate. She has been by my side though most all of the twists and turns of my life. Ag is full of love. Ag has a heart of gold and is one of the most thoughtful persons I have ever known. She is more than my wife; she is my love, my lover, my friend, my partner, my joy, the mother of my children and Gammy to my grandchildren. She can always be found at my side; she covers my back and is always there for me. She makes me laugh and she drives me crazy. She taught me all about what true unconditional love means. When she speaks her mind she is out there in her own little world. She fills me with amazing wonder in how her mind works, as she speaks her thoughts. At times I wonder if I didn't marry a clone of Mother Theresa. She talks me into things I never had the heart for. With my help she founded and runs the food pantry for our town. The pantry has been running for over 12 years. Ag and I do this work not because we seek any human praise, money or anything else. Jesus lives within us, He has given us a new nature. We are the branches and He is the vine. The vine is what produces the fruit that is displayed on the branch. He has changed our self centered nature by living within us. It is Jesus within us that produce the work that Ag and I do. We no longer live for "what's in it for us." It is now natural for us to want to help our neighbors. I can't even begin to express the wonderful joy that fills my soul to help someone else and not want anything in return. That is what Jesus is all about. God has provided us with the ability and means to provide food and other support for thousands of people in need over this time period. We step in were government agencies fail so many times due to stupid red tape regulations. We are the foot soldiers that see the need first hand in peoples lives. I kept the records for the pantry for many years, just watching God hands at work doing miracles. When the shelves were getting close to being empty or the funds were close to depletion; without solicitation, the shelves get restocked and the donations come in. This has not failed in the past 12 years. We have no paid staff, everyone volunteers. When a need arises, so does the solution.

    I also work in the pantry screening and counseling people. I will always remember this one client in particular. It was winter. This fairly attractive woman came in with two adorable pre school age children. I was to counsel her and I could not help but notice how badly someone had beaten her. She told me how embarrassed she was being at a pantry in seeking help. We hear that a lot. She said she would not have come but had nowhere else to turn. She told me this along with her story in tears. She has an abusive husband and two small children. The husband had beaten her again in a drunken rage for a stupid reason. In all the cases we see like this; there never is any reason. She told me that it was happening too often now and she could not take living like this anymore. So, she left the house with her children. The government agencies had no room for her at the time and they had placed her and the children on a waiting list. It would be at least months to years before they would be helped. The government agencies solution was to place the family in a "shelter" that is well known to us. The best description of this shelter is a large warehouse type building equipped with cots, one right next to the other. There is no privacy. There is also no discernment on who the agency places in this shelter. Here you find the most unfortunate and the most undesirable society has to offer. The drug addicts, the alcoholics, the mentally challenged, the pedophiles and the homeless coming in off the streets. The bathrooms are not private. This woman told me that she could not stay in there with her children. Instead she was living out of her car. She would park at the beach and collect cans from the trash for gas money to keep the car running for heat. She was asking for can goods that could be heated up by placing them on the car engine. I remember bringing the food out to the car. It was a junk box. It was mainly full of clothes. There were pillows and blankets. It was very clear that they were living out of this car. I gave her some money, a supermarket gift card to by milk and things we don't carry at the pantry. I also told her to please come back, we are here for her.

You read the first half of this book. I know that I would be the last one to ever admit that a self centered meatball like me could never be a Holy Roller, or some one reflecting the love that Jesus demonstrated throughout his ministry here on earth. This could not have happened to someone like me without divine intervention. God is constantly changing me. God is not done with me yet. God is doing the saving, not me; I'm still a sinner, a God rule breaker. I am simply a smuck. God put Ag in my life to help in changing my hard heart. In knowing Ag, not just knowing of her, I have learned to know how God loves unconditionally. There were so many times I would rather have my revenge, than forgive. I still can't fathom how Ag can so easily forgive when she is wronged. I'd rather hold on to the sword and get my revenge.

God has given Ag many gifts. Ag possesses the gifts of kindness, mercy, compassion, hospitality, thoughtfulness and the greatest gift of all the gift of love. I see Jesus living within my wife and doing his work through her. She shines with the fruit of Jesus' love. She is always ready to do whatever is asked of her. It's just her nature. It is what is natural for Ag to do. She's like the "ever ready" bunny; she keeps going and going and going, especially when I have long collapsed. She also sparks God to life in me. Ag is also the site manager for our town's meals on wheels program. "Meals on Wheels," delivers hot meals and also checks in on the elderly and disabled shut-ins of our town.

The Tattoo

Chapter 45

When I was a teenager I lived a fairly wild life as you might note in reading this book. One day, being very drunk, I made a wager with a couple of my buddies, who were also very drunk. The two losers of the wager had to get tattooed. As part of the wager the tattoo had to be put in a place on the body that was difficult to tattoo. Of course, I was one of the losers. I was told by the gentleman that did the tattooing that putting a tattoo on the hip was a difficult place. This was because the person being tattooed would often jump around when the needle hit the bone in this part of the body. I also decided that the tattoo would be of a "playboy bunny," as this represented my lifestyle at the time. Back then I was also in good shape and very toned. As the years passed, the bunny grew a double chin and the bunny's ears were now drooping. Every morning when I went to change or take a shower and every evening when I changed out of my shirt to get ready for bed I would always see this bunny. Whenever I would go the beach or the pool it did not fit in very well as a good witness of who I am now. It was a constant reminder of what an idiot I was.

    I checked out laser tattoo removal along with the expense. Skin grafting would still most likely still leave the tattoo outline and I would still have my memory. Jesus is the center of my life. He changed me into who I am today. In looking at the tattoo I decided that I would bury the "bunny" or "the old me" within the cross. When I entered the tattoo store I looked all around me. There were heads of all kinds of various animals hanging on the walls. There were shelves upon shelves of various dead reptiles and rodents preserved in liquid-filled jars and glass cases. There were also rows of various animal skulls. I was greeted by a man who had tattoos along with piercings, metal rings and balls covering his body. I told the man what I wanted and he said that they were not sure they could help me. I had made a drawing and asked if he could do it in free hand. He was skeptical but told me to look at the thousands of tattoos in the displays they had to see if something came close. He also told me that it would be at least an hour before someone could help me. I said I would wait and started thumbing through the displays.

During my wait many customers would enter the store. There were quite a number of mothers bringing in their daughters for tattoos or a piercing. Most of what I saw and felt was more in line with just plain evil. I felt very out of place and wondered if I should just walk out the door and forget the whole thing. I prayed about it while I was waiting hoping that God, knowing what I was planning, would give me direction. I had a feeling that I should stay and finish what I came in for. I needed to find a cross that looked more like a tree with the bark still attached. When the Romans were going to torture anyone by means of crucifixion, they would not go to the trouble of making the experience pleasant. They would not have used finely-planed or smoothly-finished wood. It would have been something made from a tree with the bark still on it just to add to the discomfort of the victim. Then, as I kept fumbling through the displays, I managed to find a cross that had the wood grain and bark that I was looking for. If it was altered just a bit it might work out.

Finally it was my turn and I showed the man the design and my drawing. I thought that maybe he could put a heart or a crown on the cross and it would then somewhat help cover the bunny. He looked at it all and told me to give him a minute to think it all out. In the meantime I was praying while I was looking all around me and at this man who was covered in tattoos and body piercings. I wondered how this man would ever understand what I was looking for. But God works through everyone and everything for good. I laughed to myself as this man said that an idea had just come to him. What if he wrapped the cross in a vine? At that very moment I remembered how Jesus called himself "the vine" and we are the branches. I said that would be perfect, but there was still one thing missing. This was not to be just any cross; it had to be the cross that meant so much to me, the cross of Jesus. I asked if the letters INRI could be put on the cross. He suggested we put it on a scroll above the cross. I said that would also be perfect.

Now when I get up every morning, or get ready for bed at night, or simply remove my shirt I am constantly reminded of "Who" is on my side, "Who" is with me and what "He" did for me. Now I smile everyday when I see that tattoo. The tattoo that has the bunny, the old me, buried within it.

The letters "INRI" in the scroll at the top of the cross stand for the initials for the Latin title that Pontius Pilate had written over the head of Jesus Christ on the cross. Latin was the official language of the Roman Empire.

The words were "Iesvs Nazarenvs Rex Ivdaeorvm." Latin uses "I" instead of the English "J," and "V" instead of "U" (i.e., Jesus Nazarenus Rex Judaeorum). The English translation is "Jesus of Nazareth, the King of the Jews." The Early Church adopted the first letters of each word of this inscription "INRI" as a symbol. Throughout the centuries INRI has appeared in many paintings of the crucifixion. Pilate's title for Christ was actually written in three languages.

In John 19:19–22 (NIV) it is stated as follows:

[19]Pilate had a notice prepared and fastened to the cross. It read: JESUS OF NAZARETH, THE KING OF THE JEWS. [20]Many of the Jews read this sign, for the place where Jesus was crucified was near the city, and the sign was written in Aramaic, Latin and Greek. [21]The chief priests of the Jews protested to Pilate, "Do not write 'The King of the Jews,' but that

this man claimed to be king of the Jews." ²²Pilate answered, "What I have written, I have written."

As for vine that surrounds the cross, it represents Jesus. In John 15: 1–8 (NIV) it is stated as follows:

¹"I am the true vine, and my Father is the gardener. ²He cuts off every branch in me that bears no fruit, while every branch that does bear fruit he prunes so that it will be even more fruitful. ³You are already clean because of the word I have spoken to you. ⁴Remain in me, and I will remain in you. No branch can bear fruit by itself; it must remain in the vine. Neither can you bear fruit unless you remain in me.

⁵"I am the vine; you are the branches. If a man remains in me and I in him, he will bear much fruit; apart from me you can do nothing. ⁶If anyone does not remain in me, he is like a branch that is thrown away and withers; such branches are picked up, thrown into the fire and burned. ⁷If you remain in me and my words remain in you, ask whatever you wish, and it will be given you. ⁸This is to my Father's glory, that you bear much fruit, showing yourselves to be my disciples.

Jesus was pierced by a spear on his side. I was pierced only by a needle on my side. Jesus suffered much, I suffered only a little.

In John 19: 33–34 (NIV) it is stated as follows:

³³But when they came to Jesus and found that he was already dead, they did not break his legs. ³⁴Instead, one of the soldiers pierced Jesus' side with a spear, bringing a sudden flow of blood and water.

In Conclusion

Chapter 46

No matter how bad life gets, no matter what obstacle is placed in your path, hang in there; trust God to show you the solution. Look what I have gone through. No matter what comes my way I can't stop trusting and loving Him. You read this book. You sized me up I was never any unblemished lamb. I wrote the first part of this book so you can see what it means to know me. But it isn't me that you need to know, you need to know Jesus. I know him and He knows me. I can't live life without Him. For all the pain and suffering I have experienced, I also have experienced many blessings. I was self centered and he taught me how to be God centered and other people centered. It makes all the difference in the world. I have prayed and He has answered me. I have frequently prayed and the answer was "no." Sometimes I have prayed and I am still waiting for the answer.

In hind sight I can clearly see God's hand all though my life. I see clearly that I am still a sinner although God has changed me quite a bit. I am still not perfect by any stretch of the imagination. God has shown me and I was given much. Jesus states that of he who is given much, much will be required. I understand clearly what God means.

Looking back on my life I can relate to some of the things Jesus and other people may have experienced. What Jesus went though was severe. I was allowed a glimpse of some of his experience. I can solemnly say to you the reader; do not let anything hinder you down here on earth from truly seeking out God and developing a personal relationship with Him. It is worth far more than any price, any sacrifice or any cross you must bear.

Please heed this wake up call. Seek the one and only one true God, you will find it will be the greatest thing you will ever do in your life and the blessings last for an eternity.

Thank You

I would first and foremost thank my Lord Jesus as I am truly unworthy for everything HE has done and is still doing for me. I would also like to thank everyone at Tate Publishing for giving me this opportunity and for all of the work and effort they all have done in publishing this book.

I would like to thank my family and friends for their love, support and encouragement. I would also like to give a special thank you to all of the individuals that took the time to read my manuscript and send me their kind thoughts and words of encouragement.

It is a rare man that allows his life to be so transparent. He is honest about his life's journey that led him to know his greatest 'Love', Jesus, the Son of the Living God, with the prayer that you, too, will give your heart to Him. May God bless this journey you have taken!

Laurel Anderson
Administrative Secretary
Division of Teacher Education
Eastern Nazarene College, Quincy, MA

I have finished your book, and was quite impressed by it. Certainly you have a lot to tell. No human being should ever have to suffer as Mark Lynch did. But thank God for the faithfulness of his wife, Agnes, who stood by his side, and for a God who is always there.

Rev. Kenneth Rayner, Retired
First Baptist Church
Braintree, MA

Walk with Me *is a book with the genuine power to stir and comfort its readers. It leads you to question one's purpose during life. In my opinion, every part of this book is quite enjoyable and I would highly recommend it to others.*

Joseph D. Thurston, M Ed.
Readjustment Counseling Therapist
Veterans Center, Brockton, MA

Mark,

I just finished reading the manuscript a week or so ago. I wanted to share with you what I thought about it.

It was very moving. I felt very touched by what I read about your life experiences. I was also interested in finding out about some of the things that you mentioned in regards to the beliefs of various religions. I, being a catholic, wanted to find out if what you were saying was true, or if this was just another "con man's" attempt to spin some facts to his benefit, to get new members to his church.

I did some research and found that EVERYTHING that you said and quoted is exactly in accordance with what the bible says. When I finished reading, I wanted to give myself a few days to sort of digest what I read, and see exactly how this was going to impact my life, because something in me was moved by what I read, and changed in some way. The bottom line is that this is not someone attempting to recruit people to join whatever religious organization you belong to, but rather a personal, moving story that tells of one man's experiences in life, and his testimony of how God found him, and he found God. The story is an inspiration to every reader to seek out a personal relationship with God. As quoted in the book, "To know Him rather than of Him".

I loved it. I am going to do something about it and how it made me feel now that I have read it, because once you know the truth, you need to seek more of it, to follow it, nurture it and live it-everyday.

Rosemary Frost, Administrative Secretary
Mortgage World Corporation, 35 Highland Circle
Needham, MA 02494

"Totally Powerful."

Mellisa Faulkner
Sophomore
Boston College, Boston, Ma.

I have just read Mark Lynches story and found it to be one of the best testimonies I have ever read! I have met Mark personally, on several occasions at a Church in Braintree, but have never heard his life story before. I could tell by talking to him, that we both graduated from the school of hard knocks, but his story is captivating! I found his book hard to put down, once I started reading it!

Mark has a great sense of humor and one thing I have always admired about him is that Mark is a straight shooter; he tells it like it is. Mark shoots from the hip and does not pull any punches. I only wish there were more people like Mark. I believe his story will be a great inspiration to many who have walked just some of the roads Mark has, and to see how God brought him to where he is at now.

I know that many of the inmates at the Correctional Facility, where I serve as Chaplin, will not only relate to Mark, but be inspired to seek out God as Mark did, and find the very meaning to life, which is Christ.

Chaplin Daniel Croce
Good News Jail & Prison Ministry
Plymouth County Correctional Facility
Plymouth, Ma.

Hey Mark,

I just read the endorsements of your book and they are so wonderful. You asked for a possible endorsement from me and after reading the endorsements that were written by a few people, I don't know if I can hold a candle to them. I will pray for the words!!

You will touch so very many people with your writing of your life. I know what a great influence you have been in my life. I knew you way back when - remember Mark, you were also the one who explained any sex questions we, the girls, all had. You answered every single one of them like a real pro.

Look at you now!!! I remember how very desperate I was for comfort, but couldn't put my finger on it. You, Mark Lynch, wouldn't let it go and kept after me about God. You were truly sent by Him to help me through my hell. If it wasn't for you and Aggie, I probably would still be there. I knew about God, the same God you knew. I feared Him because I was told to. You showed me how to let Him come into my heart. You helped me open the door because I wasn't listening to the knock. Praise the Lord for that day. From that day forward, I got to know a loving Father who sacrificed his Son for me. Me, who probably at the time broke every commandment including the two Moses, dropped. I asked myself, is this same Father who made me feel bad and guilty all of the time? You helped me to learn that I had to forgive me as God did and shed my guilt. You helped me to let Jesus carry me when I needed it, and you made me strong to stay on the road and listen to the Spirit inside of me. Mark, you truly were and still are a blessing in my life. Now, so very many years later, you have helped so many others and I know in my heart, you will be helping to guide others down a path to a brand new life.

Love, Jeanne Donahue,
Port Charlotte, FLA

Timing in Life is key. When I was presented this book I was standing at a crossroads in Life. Once I picked it up I could not place it down. I found the book entertaining but more importantly empowering. Coming from a Orthodox/Catholic religious back round I have always believed in God but have no idea who He truly is.

"Walk with me" has empowered me to want to learn, ask questions, and discover!!! Most of all is has opened my eyes to the power of FAITH. I have a long way to go but Mr. Lynch's book has given me that push in the right direction. I not only *walk with him, I keep the book close to me and read an excerpt each night. I find my FAITH and UNDERSTANDING growing everyday.*

John Metro
Senior Account Executive
Fellowship Software
New York, New York

I have known Mark Lynch and his love for Jesus Christ for 20 years, but until I read his book I did not know just how intimate and critical to his existence his relationship with the Savior is. This book reveals the ebb and flow of Mark's spiritual walk with Jesus Christ in an honest and gripping exposé of life experiences. You will see many parallels between Mark's life and the life of others recorded the Bible.

As you read this book I pray that you will drawn closer to the Savior through Marks testimony, knowing that the Savior, Jesus Christ came to all men, women and children on that they may be saved.

Thank you Mark for making your life an open book that others might be saved.

Your friend in Christ,

Jim Hoover
Braintree, Ma.

Dear Mark,

I have read your book and it is very impressive. I would like to endorse this book as a must for any one who wants to see how God's plan fits in our lives and how God makes a way that we come to the place in our lives and see His Hand guiding us. This is a personal account of a person whose story will touch any heart.

Blessings

Dr. Eleftheria Sidiropoulou
Tremont Temple, Boston, Ma.

"Walk with Me" is an amazing book of one mans journey from the darkness into the light. A story of the grace of God and the lifting of a man from despair to enlightenment, from the depths to the heights. Read and believe.

Harry B. Jones Jr.,
U.S. Army Special forces Retired

You've done a wonderful job on the book. Your story is entertaining, enlightening, and very well written.

Curtis Winkle
Conceptual Editor
Tate Publishing LLC

Contact Mark Lynch
marklynchres@comcast.net

or order more copies of this book at

TATE PUBLISHING, LLC

127 East Trade Center Terrace
Mustang, OK 73064

(888) 361 - 9473

Tate Publishing, LLC

www.tatepublishing.com